Fighting in Spain

Monte Trazo, Spain, 1937

GEORGE ORWELL

Fighting in Spain

GREAT
JOURNEYS

PENGUIN BOOKS

Published by the Penguin Group
Penguin Books Ltd, 80 Strand, London WC2R ORL, England
Penguin Group (USA) Inc., 375 Hudson Street, New York, New York 10014, USA
Penguin Group (Canada), 90 Eglinton Avenue East, Suite 700, Toronto, Ontario, Canada M4P 2Y3
(a division of Pearson Penguin Canada Inc.)
Penguin Ireland, 25 St Stephen's Green, Dublin 2, Ireland (a division of Penguin Books Ltd)
Penguin Group (Australia), 250 Camberwell Road, Camberwell, Victoria 3124, Australia
(a division of Pearson Australia Group Pty Ltd)
Penguin Books India Pvt Ltd, 11 Community Centre, Panchsheel Park, New Delhi – 110 017, India
Penguin Group (NZ), 67 Apollo Drive, Mairangi Bay, Auckland 1310, New Zealand
(a division of Pearson New Zealand Ltd)
Penguin Books (South Africa) (Pty) Ltd, 24 Sturdee Avenue, Rosebank, Johannesburg 2196, South Africa

Penguin Books Ltd, Registered Offices: 80 Strand, London WC2R ORL, England

www.penguin.com

Homage to Catalonia copyright 1938
'Looking Back on the Spanish War' copyright the Estate
of the late Sonia Brownell Orwell 1998
This extract published in Penguin Books 2007

I

Inside-cover maps by Jeff Edwards

Typeset by Rowland Phototypesetting Ltd, Bury St Edmunds, Suffolk
Printed in England by Clays Ltd, St Ives plc

ISBN: 978-0-141-02553-7

Contents

In December 1936, George Orwell (1903–1950) went to Spain to fight for the Republican side in the Spanish Civil War against Francisco Franco's Nationalist uprising. Orwell joined the POUM (Revolutionary Anti-Stalinist Communists) rather than the communist-run International Brigades by chance – but his experiences, in particular his witnessing the communist suppression of the POUM in May 1937, made him sympathetic towards the POUM and turned him into a lifelong anti-Stalinist.

I

In the Lenin Barracks in Barcelona, the day before I joined the militia, I saw an Italian militiaman standing in front of the officers' table.

He was a tough-looking youth of twenty-five or -six, with reddish yellow hair and powerful shoulders. His peaked leather cap was pulled fiercely over one eye. He was standing in profile to me, his chin on his breast, gazing with a puzzled frown at a map which one of the officers had open on the table. Something in his face deeply moved me. It was the face of a man who would commit murder and throw away his life for a friend – the kind of face you would expect in an Anarchist, though as likely as not he was a Communist. There were both candour and ferocity in it; also the pathetic reverence that illiterate people have for their supposed superiors. Obviously he could not make head or tail of the map, obviously he regarded map-reading as a stupendous intellectual feat. I hardly know why, but I have seldom seen anyone – any man, I mean – to whom I have taken such an immediate liking. While they were talking round the table some remark brought it out that I was a foreigner. The Italian raised his head and said quickly:

'Italiano?'

I answered in my bad Spanish: 'No, Inglés Y tú?' 'Italiano.'

As we went out he stepped across the room and

I

gripped my hand very hard. Queer, the affection you can feel for a stranger! It was as though his spirit and mine had momentarily succeeded in bridging the gulf of language and tradition and meeting in utter intimacy. I hoped he liked me as well as I liked him. But I also knew that to retain my first impression of him I must not see him again; and needless to say I never did see him again. One was always making contacts of that kind in Spain.

I mention this Italian militiaman because he has stuck vividly in my memory. With his shabby uniform and fierce pathetic face he typifies for me the special atmosphere of that time. He is bound up with all my memories of that period of the war – the red flags in Barcelona, the gaunt trains full of shabby soldiers creeping to the front, the grey war-stricken towns further up the line, the muddy, ice-cold trenches in the mountains.

This was in late December, 1936, less than seven months ago as I write, and yet it is a period that has already receded into enormous distance. Later events have obliterated it much more completely than they have obliterated 1935, or 1905, for that matter. I had come to Spain with some notion of writing newspaper articles, but I had joined the militia almost immediately, because at that time and in that atmosphere it seemed the only conceivable thing to do. The Anarchists were still in virtual control of Catalonia and the revolution was still in full swing. To anyone who had been there since the beginning it probably seemed even in December or January that the revolutionary period was ending; but when one came straight from England the aspect of Barcelona was something startling and overwhelming. It was the first time that I had ever been in a town where the working class was in the saddle. Practically every building of any size had been seized by the workers and was draped with red flags or with the red and black flag of the Anarchists; every wall was scrawled with the hammer and sickle and with the initials of the revolutionary parties; almost every church had been gutted and its images burnt. Churches here and there were being systematically demolished by gangs of workmen. Every shop and café had an inscription saying that it had been collectivized; even the bootblacks had been collectivized and their boxes painted red and black. Waiters and shop-walkers looked you in the face and treated you as an equal. Servile and even ceremonial forms of speech had temporarily disappeared. Nobody said '*Señor*' or '*Don*' or even '*Usted*'; everyone called everyone else '*Comrade*' and '*Thou*', and said '*Salud!*' instead of '*Buenos días*'. Almost my first experience was receiving a lecture from an hotel manager for trying to tip a lift-boy. There were no private motor cars, they had all been commandeered, and all the trams and taxis and much of the other transport were painted red and black. The revolutionary posters were everywhere, flaming from the walls in clean reds and blues that made the few remaining advertisements look like daubs of mud. Down the Ramblas, the wide central artery of the town where crowds of people streamed constantly to and fro, the loudspeakers were bellowing revolutionary songs all day and far into the night. And it was the aspect of the crowds that was the queerest thing of all. In outward appearance it was a town in which the wealthy classes had practically ceased to exist. Except for a small number of women and foreigners there were no 'well-dressed' people at all. Practically everyone wore rough working-class clothes, or blue overalls or some variant of the militia uniform. All this was queer and moving. There was much in it that I did not understand, in some ways I did not even like it, but I recognized it immediately as a state of affairs worth fighting for. Also I believed that things were as they appeared, that this was really a workers' State and that the entire bourgeoisie had either fled, been killed, or voluntarily come over to the workers' side; I did not realize that great numbers of well-to-do bourgeois were simply lying low and disguising themselves as proletarians for the time being.

Together with all this there was something of the evil atmosphere of war. The town had a gaunt untidy look, roads and buildings were in poor repair, the streets at night were dimly lit for fear of air-raids, the shops were mostly shabby and half-empty. Meat was scarce and milk practically unobtainable, there was a shortage of coal, sugar, and petrol, and a really serious shortage of bread. Even at this period the bread-queues were often hundreds of yards long. Yet so far as one could judge the people were contented and hopeful. There was no unemployment, and the price of living was still extremely low; you saw very few conspicuously destitute people, and no beggars except the gipsies.

Above all, there was a belief in the revolution and the future, a feeling of having suddenly emerged into an era of equality and freedom. Human beings were trying to behave as human beings and not as cogs in the capitalist machine. In the barbers' shops were Anarchist notices (the barbers were mostly Anarchists) solemnly explaining that barbers were no longer slaves. In the streets were coloured posters appealing to prostitutes to stop being prostitutes. To anyone from the hard-boiled, sneering civilization of the English-speaking races there was something rather pathetic in the literalness with which these idealistic Spaniards took the hackneyed phrases of revolution. At that time revolutionary ballads of the naïvest kind, all about proletarian brotherhood and the wickedness of Mussolini, were being sold on the streets for a few centimes each. I have often seen an illiterate militiaman buy one of these ballads, laboriously spell out the words, and then, when he had got the hang of it, begin singing it to an appropriate tune.

All this time I was at the Lenin Barracks, ostensibly in training for the front. When I joined the militia I had been told that I should be sent to the front the next day, but in fact I had to wait while a fresh *centuria* was got ready. The workers' militias, hurriedly raised by the trade unions at the beginning of the war, had not yet been organized on an ordinary army basis. The units of command were the 'section', of about thirty men, the *centuria*, of about a hundred men, and the 'column', which in practice meant any large number of men. The Lenin Barracks was a block of splendid stone buildings with a riding-school and enormous cobbled courtyards; it had been a cavalry barracks and had been captured during the July fighting. My *centuria* slept in one of the stables, under the stone mangers where the names of the cavalry chargers were still inscribed. All the horses had been seized and sent to the front, but the whole place still smelt of horse-piss and rotten oats. I was at the barracks about a week. Chiefly I remember the horsy smells, the quavering bugle-calls (all our buglers were amateurs – I first learned the Spanish bugle-calls by listening to them outside the Fascist lines), the tramp-tramp of hobnailed boots in the barrack yard, the long morning parades in the wintry sunshine, the wild games of football, fifty a side, in the gravelled riding-school. There were perhaps a thousand men at the barracks, and a score or so of women, apart from the militiamen's wives who did the cooking. There were still women serving in the militias, though not very many. In the early battles they had fought side by side with the men as a matter of course. It is a thing that seems natural in time of revolution. Ideas were changing already, however. The militiamen had to be kept out of the riding-school while the women were drilling there, because they laughed at the women and put them off. A few months earlier no one would have seen anything comic in a woman handling a gun.

The whole barracks was in the state of filth and chaos to which the militia reduced every building they occupied and which seems to be one of the by-products of revolution. In every corner you came upon piles of smashed furniture, broken saddles, brass cavalry-helmets, empty sabre-scabbards, and decaying food. There was frightful wastage of food, especially bread. From my barrack-room alone a basketful of bread was thrown away at every meal – a disgraceful thing when the civilian population was short of it. We ate at long trestle-tables out of permanently greasy tin pannikins, and drank out of a dreadful thing called a *porrón*. A *porrón* is a sort of glass bottle with a pointed spout from which a thin jet of wine spurts out whenever you tip it up; you can thus drink from a distance, without touching it with your lips, and it can be passed from hand to hand. I went on strike and demanded a drinking-cup as soon as I saw a *porrón* in use. To my eye the things were altogether too like bed-bottles, especially when they were filled with white wine.

By degrees they were issuing the recruits with uniforms, and because this was Spain everything was issued piecemeal, so that it was never quite certain who had received what, and various of the things we most needed, such as belts and cartridge-boxes, were not issued till the last moment when the train was actually waiting to take us to the front. I have spoken of the militia 'uniform', which probably gives a wrong impression. It was not exactly a uniform. Perhaps a 'multiform' would be the proper name for it. Everyone's clothes followed the same general plan, but they were never quite the same in any two cases. Practically everyone in the army wore corduroy knee-breeches, but there the uniformity ended. Some wore puttees, others corduroy gaiters, others leather leggings or high boots. Everyone wore a zipper jacket, but some of the jackets were of leather, others of wool and of every conceivable colour. The kinds of cap were about as numerous as their wearers. It was usual to adorn the front of your cap with a party badge, and in addition nearly every man wore a red or red and black handkerchief round his throat. A militia column at that time was an extra-ordinary-looking rabble. But the clothes had to be issued as this or that factory rushed them out, and they were not bad clothes considering the circumstances. The shirts and socks were wretched cotton things, however, quite useless against cold. I hate to think of what the militiamen must have gone through in the earlier months before anything was organized. I remember coming upon a newspaper of only about two months earlier in which one of the POUM[1] leaders, after a visit to the front, said that he would try to see to it that 'every militiaman had a blanket'. A phrase to make you shudder if you have ever slept in a trench.

On my second day at the barracks there began what was comically called 'instruction'. At the beginning there were frightful scenes of chaos. The recruits were mostly boys of sixteen or seventeen from the back streets of Barcelona, full of revolutionary ardour but completely ignorant of the meaning of war. It was impossible even to get them to stand in line. Discipline did not exist; if a man disliked an order he would step out of the ranks and argue fiercely with the officer. The lieutenant who instructed us was a stout, fresh-faced,

[1] POUM (Partido Obrero de Unificatión Marxista: Revolutionary (Anti-Stalinist) Communists).

pleasant young man who had previously been a Regular
Army officer, and still looked like one, with his smart
carriage and spick-and-span uniform. Curiously enough
he was a sincere and ardent Socialist. Even more than
the men themselves he insisted upon complete social
equality between all ranks. I remember his pained surprise when an ignorant recruit addressed him as '*Señor*'.
'What *Señor*! Who is that calling me *Señor*? Are we
not all comrades?' I doubt whether it made his job any
easier. Meanwhile the raw recruits were getting no
military training that could be of the slightest use to
them. I had been told that foreigners were not obliged
to attend 'instruction' (the Spaniards, I noticed, had a
pathetic belief that all foreigners knew more of military
matters than themselves), but naturally I turned out
with the others. I was very anxious to learn how to use
a machine-gun; it was a weapon I had never had a
chance to handle. To my dismay I found that we were
taught nothing about the use of weapons. The so-called
instruction was simply parade-ground drill of the most
antiquated, stupid kind; right turn, left turn, about
turn, marching at attention in columns of threes and
all the rest of that useless nonsense which I had learned
when I was fifteen years old. It was an extraordinary
form for the training of a guerrilla army to take. Obviously if you have only a few days in which to train a
soldier, you must teach him the things he will most
need; how to take cover, how to advance across open
ground, how to mount guards and build a parapet –
above all, how to use his weapons. Yet this mob of
eager children, who were going to be thrown into the

9

front line in a few days' time, were not even taught how to fire a rifle or pull the pin out of a bomb. At the time I did not grasp that this was because there were no weapons to be had. In the POUM militia the shortage of rifles was so desperate that fresh troops reaching the front always had to take their rifles from the troops they relieved in the line. In the whole of the Lenin Barracks there were, I believe, no rifles except those used by the sentries.

After a few days, though still a complete rabble by any ordinary standard, we were considered fit to be seen in public, and in the mornings we were marched out to the public gardens on the hill beyond the Plaza de España. This was the common drill-ground of all the party militias, besides the Carabineros and the first contingents of the newly formed Popular Army. Up in the public gardens it was a strange and heartening sight. Down every path and alleyway, amid the formal flowerbeds, squads and companies of men marched stiffly to and fro, throwing out their chests and trying desperately to look like soldiers. All of them were unarmed and none completely in uniform, though on most of them the militia uniform was breaking out in patches here and there. The procedure was always very much the same. For three hours we strutted to and fro (the Spanish marching step is very short and rapid), then we halted, broke the ranks and flocked thirstily to a little grocer's shop which was half-way down the hill and was doing a roaring trade in cheap wine. Everyone was very friendly to me. As an Englishman I was something of a curiosity, and the Carabinero officers made much of me and stood me drinks. Meanwhile, whenever I could get our lieutenant into a corner, I was clamouring to be instructed in the use of a machine-gun. I used to drag my Hugo's dictionary out of my pocket and start on him in my villainous Spanish:

'*Yo sé manejar fusil. No sé manejar ametralladora. Qutero aprender ametralladora. Quándo vamos aprender ametralladora?*'

The answer was always a harassed smile and a promise that there should be machine-gun instruction *mañana*. Needless to say *mañana* never came. Several days passed and the recruits learned to march in step and spring to attention almost smartly, but if they knew which end of a rifle the bullet came out of, that was all they knew. One day an armed Carabinero strolled up to us when we were halting and allowed us to examine his rifle. It turned out that in the whole of my section no one except myself even knew how to load the rifle, much less how to take aim.

All this time I was having the usual struggles with the Spanish language. Apart from myself there was only one Englishman at the barracks and nobody even among the officers spoke a word of French. Things were not made easier for me by the fact that when my companions spoke to one another they generally spoke in Catalan. The only way I could get along was to carry everywhere a small dictionary which I whipped out of my pocket in moments of crisis. But I would sooner be a foreigner in Spain than in most countries. How easy it is to make friends in Spain! Within a day or two there was a score of militiamen who called me by my Christian name, showed me the ropes and over-whelmed me with hospitality. I am not writing a book of propaganda and I do not want to idealize the POUM militia. The whole militia-system had serious faults, and the men themselves were a mixed lot, for by this time voluntary recruitment was falling off and many of the best men were already at the front or dead. There was always among us a certain percentage who were completely useless. Boys of fifteen were being brought up for enlistment by their parents, quite openly for the sake of the ten pesetas a day which was the militiaman's wage; also for the sake of the bread which the militia received in plenty and could smuggle home to their parents. But I defy anyone to be thrown as I was among the Spanish working class – I ought perhaps to say the Catalan working class, for apart from a few Aragónese and Andalusians I mixed only with Catalans – and not be struck by their essential decency; above all, their straightforwardness and generosity. A Spaniard's generosity, in the ordinary sense of the word, is at times almost embarrassing. If you ask him for a cigarette he will force the whole packet upon you. And beyond this there is generosity in a deeper sense, a real largeness of spirit, which I have met with again and again in the most unpromising circumstances. Some of the journal-ists and other foreigners who travelled in Spain during the war have declared that in secret the Spaniards were bitterly jealous of foreign aid. All I can say is that I never observed anything of the kind. I remember that a few days before I left the barracks a group of men returned on leave from the front. They were talking excitedly about their experiences and were full of enthusiasm for some French troops who had been next to them at Huesca. The French were very brave, they said; adding enthusiastically: '*Más valientes que nosotros*' – 'Braver than we are!' Of course I demurred, whereupon they explained that the French knew more of the art of war – were more expert with bombs, machine-guns, and so forth. Yet the remark was significant. An Englishman would cut his hand off sooner than say a thing like that.

Every foreigner who served in the militia spent his first few weeks in learning to love the Spaniards and in being exasperated by certain of their characteristics. In the front line my own exasperation sometimes reached the pitch of fury. The Spaniards are good at many things, but not at making war. All foreigners alike are appalled by their inefficiency, above all their maddening unpunctuality. The one Spanish word that no foreigner can avoid learning is *mañana* – 'to-morrow' (literally, 'the morning'). Whenever it is conceivably possible, the business of today is put off until *mañana*. This is so notorious that even the Spaniards themselves make jokes about it. In Spain nothing, from a meal to a battle, ever happens at the appointed time. As a general rule things happen too late, but just occasionally – just so that you shan't even be able to depend on their happening late – they happen too early. A train which is due to leave at eight will normally leave at any time between nine and ten, but perhaps once a week, thanks to some private whim of the engine-driver, it leaves at half-past seven. Such things can be a little trying. In theory I rather admire the Spaniards for not sharing our Northern time-neurosis, but unfortunately I share it myself.

After endless rumours, *mañanas*, and delays we were suddenly ordered to the front at two hours' notice, when much of our equipment was still unissued. There were terrible tumults in the quartermaster's store, in the end numbers of men had to leave without their full equipment. The barracks had promptly filled with women who seemed to have sprung up from the ground and were helping their menfolk to roll their blankets and pack their kit-bags. It was rather humiliating that I had to be shown how to put on my new leather cartridge-boxes by a Spanish girl, the wife of Williams, the other English militiaman. She was a gentle, dark-eyed, intensely feminine creature who looked as though her life-work was to rock a cradle, but who as a matter of fact had fought bravely in the street-battles of July. At this time she was carrying a baby which was born just ten months after the outbreak of war and had perhaps been begotten behind a barricade.

The train was due to leave at eight, and it was about ten past eight when the harassed, sweating officers managed to marshal us in the barrack square. I remember very vividly the torchlit scene – the uproar and excitement, the red flags flapping in the torchlight, the massed ranks of militiamen with their knapsacks on their backs and their rolled blankets worn bandolier-wise across the shoulder; and the shouting and the clatter of boots and tin pannikins, and then a tremendous and finally successful hissing for silence; and then some political commissar standing beneath a huge rolling red banner and making us a speech in Catalan. Finally they marched us to the station, taking the longest route, three or four miles, so as to show us to the whole town. In the Ramblas they halted us while a borrowed band played some revolutionary tune or other. Once again the conquering-hero stuff – shouting and enthusiasm, red flags and red and black flags everywhere, friendly crowds thronging the pavement to have a look at us, women waving from the windows. How natural it all seemed then; how remote and improbable now! The train was packed so tight with men that there was barely room even on the floor, let alone on the seats. At the last moment Williams's wife came rushing down the platform and gave us a bottle of wine and a foot of that bright red sausage which tastes of soap and gives you diarrhoea. The train crawled out of Catalonia and on to the plateau of Aragón at the normal war-time speed of something under twenty kilometres an hour.

II

Barbastro, though a long way from the front line, looked bleak and chipped. Swarms of militiamen in shabby uniforms wandered up and down the streets, trying to keep warm. On a ruinous wall I came upon a poster dating from the previous year and announcing that 'six handsome bulls' would be killed in the arena on such and such a date. How forlorn its faded colours looked! Where were the handsome bulls and the hand-some bullfighters now? It appeared that even in Bar-celona there were hardly any bullfights nowadays; for some reason all the best matadors were Fascists.

They sent my company by lorry to Siétamo, then westward to Alcubierre, which was just behind the line fronting Saragossa. Siétamo had been fought over three times before the Anarchists finally took it in October, and parts of it were smashed to pieces by shell-fire and most of the houses pockmarked by rifle-bullets. We were 1,500 feet above sea-level now. It was beastly cold, with dense mists that came swirling up from nowhere. Between Siétamo and Alcubierre the lorry-driver lost his way (this was one of the regular features of the war) and we were wandering for hours in the mist. It was late at night when we reached Alcubierre. Somebody shepherded us through morasses of mud into a mule-stable where we dug ourselves down into the chaff and promptly fell asleep. Chaff is not bad to sleep in when it is clean, not so good as hay but better than straw. It was only in the morning light that I discovered that the chaff was full of breadcrusts, torn newspaper, bones, dead rats, and jagged milk tins.

We were near the front line now, near enough to smell the characteristic smell of war – in my experience a smell of excrement and decaying food. Alcubierre had never been shelled and was in a better state than most of the villages immediately behind the line. Yet I believe that even in peacetime you could not travel in that part of Spain without being struck by the peculiar squalid misery of the Aragonese villages. They are built like fortresses, a mass of mean little houses of mud and stone huddling round the church, and even in spring you see hardly a flower anywhere; the houses have no gardens, only backyards where ragged fowls skate over the beds of mule-dung. It was vile weather, with alternate mist and rain. The narrow earth roads had been churned into a sea of mud, in places two feet deep, through which the lorries struggled with racing wheels and the peasants led their clumsy carts which were pulled by strings of mules, sometimes as many as six in a string, always pulling tandem. The constant come-and-go of troops had reduced the village to a state of unspeakable filth. It did not possess and never had possessed such a thing as a lavatory or a drain of any kind, and there was not a square yard anywhere where you could tread without watching your step. The church had long been used as a latrine; so had all the fields for a quarter of a mile round. I never think of my first two months at war without thinking of wintry stubble fields whose edges are crusted with dung.

Two days passed and no rifles were issued to us. When you had been to the Comité de Guerra and inspected the row of holes in the wall – holes made by rifle-volleys, various Fascist having been executed there – you had seen all the sights that Alcubierre contained. Up in the front line things were obviously quiet; very few wounded were coming in. The chief excitement was the arrival of Fascist deserters, who were brought under guard from the front line. Many of the troops opposite us on this part of the line were not Fascists at all, merely wretched conscripts who had been doing

their military service at the time when war broke
out and were only too anxious to escape. Occasionally
small batches of them took the risk of slipping across
to our lines. No doubt more would have done so if
their relatives had not been in Fascist territory. These
deserters were the first 'real' Fascists I had ever seen.
It struck me that they were indistinguishable from
ourselves, except that they wore khaki overalls. They
were always ravenously hungry when they arrived –
natural enough after a day or two of dodging about in
no-man's-land, but it was always triumphantly pointed
to as a proof that the Fascist troops were starving. I
watched one of them being fed in a peasant's house. It
was somehow rather a pitiful sight. A tall boy of twenty,
deeply windburnt, with his clothes in rags, crouched
over the fire shovelling a pannikinful of stew into himself at desperate speed; and all the while his eyes flitted
nervously round the ring of militiamen who stood
watching him. I think he still half-believed that we
were bloodthirsty 'Reds' and were going to shoot
him as soon as he had finished his meal; the armed
man who guarded him kept stroking his shoulder and
making reassuring noises. On one memorable day fifteen deserters arrived in a single batch. They were led
through the village in triumph with a man riding in
front of them on a white horse. I managed to take a
rather blurry photograph which was stolen from me
later.

On our third morning in Alcubierre the rifles
arrived. A sergeant with a coarse dark-yellow face was
handing them out in the mule-stable. I got a shock of

dismay when I saw the thing they gave me. It was a German Mauser dated 1896 – more than forty years old! It was rusty, the bolt was stiff, the wooden barrel-guard was split; one glance down the muzzle showed that it was corroded and past praying for. Most of the rifles were equally bad, some of them even worse, and no attempt was made to give the best weapons to the men who knew how to use them. The best rifle of the lot, only ten years old, was given to a half-witted little beast of fifteen, known to everyone as the *maricón* (Nancy-boy). The sergeant gave us five minutes' 'instruction', which consisted in explaining how you loaded a rifle and how you took the bolt to pieces. Many of the militiamen had never had a gun in their hands before, and very few, I imagine, knew what the sights were for. Cartridges were handed out, fifty to a man, and then the ranks were formed and we strapped our kits on our backs and set out for the front line, about three miles away.

The *centuria*, eighty men and several dogs, wound raggedly up the road. Every militia column had at least one dog attached to it as a mascot. One wretched brute that marched with us had had POUM branded on it in huge letters and slunk along as though conscious that there was something wrong with its appearance. At the head of the column, beside the red flag, Georges Kopp, the stout Belgian *comandante*, was riding a black horse; a little way ahead a youth from the brigand-like militia cavalry pranced to and fro, galloping up every piece of rising ground and posing himself in picturesque attitudes at the summit. The splendid horses of the Spanish cavalry had been captured in large numbers during the revolution and handed over to the militia, who, of course, were busy riding them to death.

The road wound between yellow infertile fields, untouched since last year's harvest. Ahead of us was the low sierra that lies between Alcubierre and Saragossa. We were getting near the front line now, near the bombs, the machine-guns and the mud. In secret I was frightened. I knew the line was quiet at present, but unlike most of the men about me I was old enough to remember the Great War, though not old enough to have fought in it. War, to me, meant roaring projectiles and skipping shards of steel; above all it meant mud, lice, hunger, and cold. It is curious, but I dreaded the cold much more than I dreaded the enemy. The thought of it had been haunting me all the time I was in Barcelona; I had even lam awake at nights thinking of the cold in the trenches, the stand-to's in the grisly dawns, the long hours on sentry-go with a frosted rifle, the icy mud that would slop over my boot-tops. I admit, too, that I felt a kind of horror as I looked at the people I was marching among. You cannot possibly conceive what a rabble we looked. We straggled along with far less cohesion than a flock of sheep; before we had gone two miles the rear of the column was out of sight. And quite half of the so-called men were children – but I mean literally children, of sixteen years old at the very most. Yet they were all happy and excited at the prospect of getting to the front at last. As we neared the line the boys round the red flag in front began to utter shouts of *'Visca POUM!' 'Fascistas* –

maricones!' and so forth – shouts which were meant
to be war-like and menacing, but which, from those
childish throats, sounded as pathetic as the cries of
kittens. It seemed dreadful that the defenders of the
Republic should be this mob of ragged children carrying worn-out rifles which they did not know how to
use. I remember wondering what would happen if a
Fascist aeroplane passed our way – whether the airman
would even bother to dive down and give us a burst
from his machine-gun. Surely even from the air he
could see that we were not real soldiers?

As the road struck into the sierra we branched off
to the right and climbed a narrow mule-track that
wound round the mountain-side. The hills in that part
of Spain are of a queer formation, horseshoe-shaped
with flattish tops and very steep sides running down
into immense ravines. On the higher slopes nothing
grows except stunted shrubs and heath, with the white
bones of the limestone sticking out everywhere. The
front line here was not a continuous line of trenches,
which would have been impossible in such mountain-
ous country; it was simply a chain of fortified posts,
always known as 'positions', perched on each hilltop.
In the distance you could see our 'position' at the crown
of the horseshoe; a ragged barricade of sandbags, a red
flag fluttering, the smoke of dug-out fires. A little
nearer, and you could smell a sickening sweetish stink
that lived in my nostrils for weeks afterwards. Into the
cleft immediately behind the position all the refuse of
months had been tipped – a deep festering bed of
breadcrusts, excrement, and rusty tins.

The company we were relieving were getting their kits together. They had been three months in the line; their uniforms were caked with mud, their boots falling to pieces, their faces mostly bearded. The captain commanding the position, Levinski by name, but known to everyone as Benjamin, and by birth a Polish Jew, but speaking French as his native language, crawled out of his dug-out and greeted us. He was a short youth of about twenty-five, with stiff black hair and a pale eager face which at this period of the war was always very dirty. A few stray bullets were cracking high overhead. The position was a semi-circular enclosure about fifty yards across, with a parapet that was partly sandbags and partly lumps of limestone. There were thirty or forty dug-outs running into the ground like rat-holes. Williams, myself, and Williams's Spanish brother-in-law made a swift dive for the nearest unoccupied dug-out that looked habitable. Somewhere in front an occasional rifle banged, making queer rolling echoes among the stony hills. We had just dumped our kits and were crawling out of the dug-out when there was another bang and one of the children of our company rushed back from the parapet with his face pouring blood. He had fired his rifle and had somehow managed to blow out the bolt; his scalp was torn to ribbons by the splinters of the burst cartridge-case. It was our first casualty, and, characteristically, self-inflicted.

In the afternoon we did our first guard and Benjamin showed us round the position. In front of the parapet there ran a system of narrow trenches hewn out of the rock, with extremely primitive loopholes made of piles of limestone. There were twelve sentries, placed at various points in the trench and behind the inner parapet. In front of the trench was the barbed wire, and then the hill-side slid down into a seemingly bottomless ravine; opposite were naked hills, in places mere cliffs of rock, all grey and wintry, with no life anywhere, not even a bird. I peered cautiously through a loophole, trying to find the Fascist trench.

'Where are the enemy?'

Benjamin waved his hand expansively. 'Over zere.' (Benjamin spoke English – terrible English.)

'But *where*?'

According to my ideas of trench warfare the Fascists would be fifty or a hundred yards away. I could see nothing – seemingly these trenches were very well concealed. Then with a shock of dismay I saw where Benjamin was pointing; on the opposite hill-top, beyond the ravine, seven hundred metres away at the very least, the tiny outline of a parapet and a red-and-yellow flag – the Fascist position. I was indescribably disappointed. We were nowhere near them! At that range our rifles were completely useless. But at this moment there was a shout of excitement. Two Fascists, greyish figurines in the distance, were scrambling up the naked hill-side opposite. Benjamin grabbed the nearest man's rifle, took aim, and pulled the trigger. Click! A dud cartridge; I thought it a bad omen.

The new sentries were no sooner in the trench than they began firing a terrific fusillade at nothing in particular. I could see the Fascists, tiny as ants, dodging to and fro behind their parapet, and sometimes a black dot which was a head would pause for a moment, impudently exposed. It was obviously no use firing. But presently the sentry on my left, leaving his post in the typical Spanish fashion, sidled up to me and began urging me to fire. I tried to explain that at that range and with these rifles you could not hit a man except by accident. But he was only a child, and he kept motioning with his rifle towards one of the dots, grinning as eagerly as a dog that expects a pebble to be thrown. Finally I put my sights up to seven hundred and let fly. The dot disappeared. I hope it went near enough to make him jump. It was the first time in my life that I had fired a gun at a human being.

Now that I had seen the front I was profoundly disgusted. They called this war! And we were hardly even in touch with the enemy! I made no attempt to keep my head below the level of the trench. A little while later, however, a bullet shot past my ear with a vicious crack and banged into the parados behind. Alas! I ducked. All my life I had sworn that I would not duck the first time a bullet passed over me; but the movement appears to be instinctive, and almost everybody does it at least once.

III

In trench warfare five things are important: firewood, food, tobacco, candles and the enemy. In winter on the Saragossa front they were important in that order, with the enemy a bad last. Except at night, when a surprise-attack was always conceivable, nobody bothered about the enemy. They were simply remote black insects whom one occasionally saw hopping to and fro. The real preoccupation of both armies was trying to keep warm.

I ought to say in passing that all the time I was in Spain I saw very little fighting. I was on the Aragón front from January to May, and between January and late March little or nothing happened on that front, except at Teruel. In March there was heavy fighting round Huesca, but I personally played only a minor part in it. Later, in June, there was the disastrous attack on Huesca in which several thousand men were killed in a single day, but I had been wounded and disabled before that happened. The things that one normally thinks of as the horrors of war seldom happened to me. No aeroplane ever dropped a bomb anywhere near me, I do not think a shell ever exploded within fifty yards of me, and I was only in hand-to-hand fighting once (once is once too often, I may say). Of course I was often under heavy machine-gun fire, but usually at longish ranges. Even at Huesca you were generally safe enough if you took reasonable precautions.

Up here, in the hills round Saragossa, it was simply the mingled boredom and discomfort of stationary warfare. A life as uneventful as a city clerk's, and almost as regular. Sentry-go, patrols, digging; digging, patrols, sentry-go. On every hill-top, Fascist or Loyalist, a knot of ragged, dirty men shivering round their flag and trying to keep warm. And all day and night the

meaningless bullets wandering across the empty valleys
and only by some rare improbable chance getting home
on a human body.

Often I used to gaze round the wintry landscape and
marvel at the futility of it all. The inconclusiveness of
such a kind of war! Earlier, about October, there had
been savage fighting for all these hills; then, because
the lack of men and arms, especially artillery, made any
large-scale operation impossible, each army had dug
itself in and settled down on the hill-tops it had won.
Over to our right there was a small outpost, also
POUM, and on the spur to our left, at seven o'clock
of us, a PSUC,[2] position faced a taller spur with several
small Fascist posts dotted on its peaks. The so-called
line zigzagged to and fro in a pattern that would have
been quite unintelligible if every position had not flown
a flag. The POUM and PSUC flags were red, those
of the Anarchists red and black; the Fascists generally
flew the monarchist flag (red-yellow-red) but occasionally they flew the flag of the Republic (red-yellow-
purple). The scenery was stupendous, if you could
forget that every mountain-top was occupied by troops
and was therefore littered with tin cans and crusted
with dung. To the right of us the sierra bent south-
eastwards and made way for the wide, veined valley
that stretched across to Huesca. In the middle of the
plain a few tiny cubes sprawled like a throw of dice;
this was the town of Robres, which was in Loyalist

[2] PSUC (Partido Socialista Unificado de Cataluña; United Catalan
Socialist Party = Catalan Communists).

possession. Often in the mornings the valley was hidden under seas of cloud, out of which the hills rose flat and blue, giving the landscape a strange resemblance to a photographic negative. Beyond Huesca there were more hills of the same formation as our own, streaked with a pattern of snow which altered day by day. In the far distance the monstrous peaks of the Pyrenees, where the snow never melts, seemed to float upon nothing. Even down in the plain everything looked dead and bare. The hills opposite us were grey and wrinkled like the skins of elephants. Almost always the sky was empty of birds. I do not think I have ever seen a country where there were so few birds. The only birds one saw at any time were a kind of magpie, and the coveys of partridges that startled one at night with their sudden whirring, and, very rarely, the flights of eagles that drifted slowly over, generally followed by rifle-shots which they did not deign to notice.

At night and in misty weather patrols were sent out in the valley between ourselves and the Fascists. The job was not popular, it was too cold and too easy to get lost, and I soon found that I could get leave to go out on patrol as often as I wished. In the huge jagged ravines there were no paths or tracks of any kind; you could only find your way about by making successive journeys and noting fresh landmarks each time. As the bullet flies the nearest Fascist post was seven hundred metres from our own, but it was a mile and a half by the only practicable route. It was rather fun wandering about the dark valleys with the stray bullets flying high overhead like redshanks whistling. Better than night-time were the heavy mists, which often lasted all day and which had a habit of clinging round the hill-tops and leaving the valleys clear. When you were anywhere near the Fascist lines you had to creep at a snail's pace; it was very difficult to move quietly on those hill-sides, among the crackling shrubs and tinkling limestones. It was only at the third or fourth attempt that I managed to find my way to the Fascist lines. The mist was very thick, and I crept up to the barbed wire to listen. I could hear the Fascists talking and singing inside. Then to my alarm I heard several of them coming down the hill towards me. I cowered behind a bush that suddenly seemed very small, and tried to cock my rifle without noise. However, they branched off and did not come within sight of me. Behind the bush where I was hiding I came upon various relics of the earlier fighting – a pile of empty cartridge-cases, a leather cap with a bullet-hole in it, and a red flag, obviously one of our own. I took it back to the position, where it was unsentimentally torn up for cleaning-rags.

I had been made a corporal, or *cabo*, as it was called, as soon as we reached the front, and was in command of a guard of twelve men. It was no sinecure, especially at first. The *centuria* was an untrained mob composed mostly of boys in their teens. Here and there in the militia you came across children as young as eleven or twelve, usually refugees from Fascist territory who had been enlisted as militiamen as the easiest way of providing for them. As a rule they were employed on light work in the rear, but sometimes they managed to worm their way to the front line, where they were a public menace. I remember one little brute throwing a hand-grenade into the dug-out fire 'for a joke'. At Monte Pocero I do not think there was anyone younger than fifteen, but the average age must have been well under twenty. Boys of this age ought never to be used in the front line, because they cannot stand the lack of sleep which is inseparable from trench warfare. At the beginning it was almost impossible to keep our position properly guarded at night. The wretched children of my section could only be roused by dragging them out of their dugouts feet foremost, and as soon as your back was turned they left their posts and slipped into shelter; or they would even, in spite of the frightful cold, lean up against the wall of the trench and fall fast asleep. Luckily the enemy were very unenterprising. There were nights when it seemed to me that our position could be stormed by twenty Boy Scouts armed with air-guns, or twenty Girl Guides armed with battledores for that matter.

At this time and until much later the Catalan militias were still on the same basis as they had been at the beginning of the war. In the early days of Franco's revolt the militias had been hurriedly raised by the various trade unions and political parties; each was essentially a political organization, owing allegiance to its party as much as to the central Government. When the Popular Army, which was a 'non-political' army organized on more or less ordinary lines, was raised at the beginning of 1937, the party militias were theoretically incorporated in it. But for a long time the only changes that occurred were on paper; the new Popular Army troops did not reach the Aragón front in any numbers till June, and until that time the militia-system remained unchanged. The essential point of the system was social equality between officers and men. Everyone from general to private drew the same pay, ate the same food, wore the same clothes, and mingled on terms of complete equality. If you wanted to slap the general commanding the division on the back and ask him for a cigarette, you could do so, and no one thought it curious. In theory at any rate each militia was a democracy and not a hierarchy. It was understood that orders had to be obeyed, but it was also understood that when you gave an order you gave it as comrade to comrade and not as superior to inferior. There were officers and NCOs, but there was no military rank in the ordinary sense; no titles, no badges, no heel-clicking and saluting. They had attempted to produce within the militias a sort of temporary working model of the classless society. Of course there was not perfect equality, but there was a nearer approach to it than I had ever seen or than I would have thought conceivable in time of war.

But I admit that at first sight the state of affairs at the front horrified me. How on earth could the war be won by an army of this type? It was what everyone was saying at the time, and though it was true it was also unreasonable. For in the circumstances the militias could not have been much better than they were. A modern mechanized army does not spring up out of the ground, and if the Government had waited until it had trained troops at its disposal, Franco would never have been resisted. Later it became the fashion to decry the militias, and therefore to pretend that the faults which were due to lack of training and weapons were the result of the equalitarian system. Actually, a newly raised draft of militia was an undisciplined mob not because the officers called the privates 'Comrade' but because raw troops are *always* an undisciplined mob. In practice the democratic 'revolutionary' type of discipline is more reliable than might be expected. In a workers' army discipline is theoretically voluntary. It is based on class-loyalty, whereas the discipline of a bourgeois conscript army is based ultimately on fear. (The Popular Army that replaced the militias was midway between the two types.) In the militias the bullying and abuse that go on in an ordinary army would never have been tolerated for a moment. The normal military punishments existed, but they were only invoked for very serious offences. When a man refused to obey an order you did not immediately get him punished; you first appealed to him in the name of comradeship. Cynical people with no experience of handling men will say instantly that this would never 'work', but as a matter of fact it does 'work' in the long run. The discipline of even the worst drafts of militia visibly improved as time went on. In January the job of keeping a dozen raw recruits up to the mark almost turned my hair grey. In May for a short while I was acting-lieutenant in command of about thirty men, English and Spanish. We had all been under fire for months, and I never had the slightest difficulty in getting an order obeyed or in getting men to volunteer for a dangerous job. 'Revolutionary' discipline depends on political consciousness – on an understanding of *why* orders must be obeyed; it takes time to diffuse this, but it also takes time to drill a man into an automaton on the barrack-square. The journalists who sneered at the militia-system seldom remembered that the militias had to hold the line while the Popular Army was training in the rear. And it is a tribute to the strength of 'revolutionary' discipline that the militias stayed in the field at all. For until about June 1937 there was nothing to keep them there, except class loyalty. Individual deserters could be shot – were shot, occasionally – but if a thousand men had decided to walk out of the line together there was no force to stop them. A conscript army in the same circumstances – with its battle-police removed – would have melted away. Yet the militias held the line, though God knows they won very few victories, and even individual desertions were not common. In four or five months in the POUM militia I only heard of four men deserting, and two of those were fairly certainly spies who had enlisted to obtain information. At the beginning the apparent chaos, the general lack of training, the fact that you often had to argue for five minutes before you could get an order obeyed, appalled and infuriated me. I had British Army ideas, and certainly the Spanish militias were very unlike the British Army. But considering the circumstances they were better troops than one had any right to expect.

Meanwhile, firewood – always firewood. Throughout that period there is probably no entry in my diary that does not mention firewood, or rather the lack of it. We were between two and three thousand feet above sea-level, it was mid-winter and the cold was unspeakable. The temperature was not exceptionally low, on many nights it did not even freeze, and the wintry sun often shone for an hour in the middle of the day, but even if it was not really cold, I assure you that it seemed so. Sometimes there were shrieking winds that tore your cap off and twisted your hair in all directions, sometimes there were mists that poured into the trench like a liquid and seemed to penetrate your bones; frequently it rained, and even a quarter of an hour's rain was enough to make conditions intolerable. The thin skin of earth over the limestone turned promptly into a slippery grease, and as you were always walking on a slope it was impossible to keep your footing. On dark nights I have often fallen half a dozen times in twenty yards; and this was dangerous, because it meant that the lock of one's rifle became jammed with mud. For days together clothes, boots, blankets, and rifles were more or less coated with mud. I had brought as many thick clothes as I could carry, but many of the men were terribly underclad. For the whole garrison, about a hundred men, there were only twelve greatcoats, which had to be handed from sentry to sentry, and most of the men had only one blanket. One icy night I made a list in my diary of the clothes I was wearing. It is of some interest as showing the amount of clothes the human body can carry. I was wearing a thick vest and pants, a flannel shirt, two pullovers, a woollen jacket, a pigskin jacket, corduroy breeches, puttees, thick socks, boots, a stout trench-coat, a muffler, lined leather gloves, and a woollen cap. Nevertheless I was shivering like a jelly. But I admit I am unusually sensitive to cold.

Firewood was the one thing that really mattered. The point about the firewood was that there was practically no firewood to be had. Our miserable mountain had not even at its best much vegetation, and for months it had been ranged over by freezing militiamen, with the result that everything thicker than one's finger had long since been burnt. When we were not eating, sleeping, on guard or on fatigue-duty we were in the valley behind the position, scrounging for fuel. All my memories of that time are memories of scrambling up and down the almost perpendicular slopes, over the jagged limestone that knocked one's boots to pieces, pouncing eagerly on tiny twigs of wood. Three people searching for a couple of hours could collect enough fuel to keep the dug-out fire alight for about an hour. The eagerness of our search for firewood turned us all into botanists. We classified according to their burning qualities every plant that grew on the mountain-side; the various heaths and grasses that were good to start a fire with but burnt out in a few minutes, the wild rosemary and the tiny whin bushes that would burn when the fire was well alight, the stunted oak tree, smaller than a gooseberry bush, that was practically unburnable. There was a kind of dried-up reed that was very good for starting fires with, but these grew only on the hill-top to the left of the position, and you had to go under fire to get them. If the Fascist machine-gunners saw you they gave you a drum of ammunition all to yourself. Generally their aim was high and the bullets sang overhead like birds, but sometimes they crackled and chipped the limestone uncomfortably close, whereupon you flung yourself on your face. You went on gathering reeds, however; nothing mattered in comparison with firewood.

Beside the cold the other discomforts seemed petty. Of course all of us were permanently dirty. Our water, like our food, came on mule-back from Alcubierre, and each man's share worked out at about a quart a day. It was beastly water, hardly more transparent than milk. Theoretically it was for drinking only, but I always stole a pannikinful for washing in the mornings. I used to wash one day and shave the next: there was never enough water for both. The position stank abominably, and outside the little enclosure of the barricade there was excrement everywhere. Some of the militiamen habitually defecated in the trench, a disgusting thing when one had to walk round it in the darkness. But the dirt never worried me. Dirt is a thing people make too much fuss about. It is astonishing how quickly you get used to doing without a handkerchief and to eating out of the tin pannikin in which you also wash. Nor was sleeping in one's clothes any hardship after a day or two. It was of course impossible to take one's clothes and especially one's boots off at night, one had to be ready to turn out instantly in case of an attack. In eighty nights I only took my clothes off three times, though I did occasionally manage to get them off in the daytime. It was too cold for lice as yet, but rats and mice abounded. It is often said that you don't find rats and mice in the same place, but you do when there is enough food for them.

In other ways we were not badly off. The food was good enough and there was plenty of wine. Cigarettes were still being issued at the rate of a packet a day, matches were issued every other day, and there was even an issue of candles. They were very thin candles, like those on a Christmas cake, and were popularly supposed to have been looted from churches. Every dug-out was issued daily with three inches of candle, which would burn for about twenty minutes. At that time it was still possible to buy candles, and I had brought several pounds of them with me. Later on the famine of matches and candles made life a misery. You do not realize the importance of these things until you lack them. In a night-alarm, for instance, when everyone in the dug-out is scrambling for his rifle and treading on everybody else's face, being able to strike a light may make the difference between life and death. Every militiaman possessed a tinder-lighter and several yards of yellow wick. Next to his rifle it was his most important possession. The tinder-lighters had the great advantage that they could be struck in a wind, but they would only smoulder, so that they were no use for lighting a fire. When the match famine was at its worst our only way of producing a flame was to pull the bullet out of a cartridge and touch the cordite off with a tinder-lighter.

It was an extraordinary life that we were living – an

extraordinary way to be at war, if you could call it war. The whole militia chafed against the inaction and clamoured constantly to know why we were not allowed to attack. But it was perfectly obvious that there would be no battle for a long while yet, unless the enemy started it. Georges Kopp, on his periodical tours of inspection, was quite frank with us. 'This is not a war,' he used to say, 'it is a comic opera with an occasional death.' As a matter of fact the stagnation on the Aragón front had political causes of which I knew nothing at that time; but the purely military difficulties – quite apart from the lack of reserves of men – were obvious to anybody.

To begin with, there was the nature of the country. The front line, ours and the Fascists', lay in positions of immense natural strength, which as a rule could only be approached from one side. Provided a few trenches have been dug, such places cannot be taken by infantry, except in overwhelming numbers. In our own position or most of those round us a dozen men with two machine-guns could have held off a battalion. Perched on the hill-tops as we were, we should have made lovely marks for artillery; but there was no artillery. Sometimes I used to gaze round the landscape and long – oh, how passionately! – for a couple of batteries of guns. One could have destroyed the enemy positions one after another as easily as smashing nuts with a hammer. But on our side the guns simply did not exist. The Fascists did occasionally manage to bring a gun or two from Saragossa and fire a very few shells, so few that they never even found the range and the shells plunged harmlessly into the empty ravines. Against machine-guns and without artillery there are only three things you can do: dig yourself in at a safe distance – four hundred yards, say – advance across the open and be massacred, or make small-scale night-attacks that will not alter the general situation. Practically the alternatives are stagnation or suicide.

And beyond this there was the complete lack of war materials of every description. It needs an effort to realize how badly the militias were armed at this time. Any public school OTC in England is far more like a modern army than we were. The badness of our weapons was so astonishing that it is worth recording in detail.

For this sector of the front the entire artillery consisted of four trench-mortars with *fifteen rounds* for each gun. Of course they were far too precious to be fired and the mortars were kept in Alcubierre. There were machine-guns at the rate of approximately one to fifty men; they were oldish guns, but fairly accurate up to three or four hundred yards. Beyond this we had only rifles, and the majority of the rifles were scrap-iron. There were three types of rifle in use. The first was the long Mauser. These were seldom less than twenty years old, their sights were about as much use as a broken speedometer, and in most of them the rifling was hopelessly corroded; about one rifle in ten was not bad, however. Then there was the short Mauser, or *mousqueton*, really a cavalry weapon. These were more popular than the others because they were lighter to carry and less nuisance in a trench, also because they were comparatively new and looked efficient. Actually they were almost useless. They were made out of reassembled parts, no bolt belonged to its rifle, and three-quarters of them could be counted on to jam after five shots. There were also a few Winchester rifles. These were nice to shoot with, but they were waldly inaccurate, and as their cartridges had no clips they could only be fired one shot at a time. Ammunition was so scarce that each man entering the line was only issued with fifty rounds, and most of it was exceedingly bad. The Spanish-made cartridges were all refills and would jam even the best rifles. The Mexican cartridges were better and were therefore reserved for the machine-guns. Best of all was the German-made ammunition, but as this came only from prisoners and deserters there was not much of it. I always kept a clip of German or Mexican ammunition in my pocket for use in an emergency. But in practice when the emergency came I seldom fired my rifle; I was too frightened of the beastly thing jamming and too anxious to reserve at any rate one round that would go off.

We had no tin hats, no bayonets, hardly any revolvers or pistols, and not more than one bomb between five or ten men. The bomb in use at this time was a frightful object known as the 'FAI bomb', it having been produced by the Anarchists in the early days of the war. It was on the principle of a Mills bomb, but the lever was held down not by a pin but a piece of tape. You broke the tape and then got rid of the bomb with the utmost possible speed. It was said of these bombs that they were 'impartial'; they killed the man they were thrown at and the man who threw them. There were several other types, even more primitive but probably a little less dangerous – to the thrower, I mean. It was not till late March that I saw a bomb worth throwing.

And apart from weapons there was a shortage of all the minor necessities of war. We had no maps or charts, for instance. Spain has never been fully surveyed, and the only detailed maps of this area were the old military ones, which were almost all in the possession of the Fascists. We had no range-finders, no telescopes, no periscopes, no field-glasses except a few privately-owned pairs, no flares or Very lights, no wire-cutters, no armourers' tools, hardly even any cleaning materials. The Spaniards seemed never to have heard of a pull-through and looked on in surprise when I constructed one. When you wanted your rifle cleaned you took it to the sergeant, who possessed a long brass ramrod which was invariably bent and therefore scratched the rifling. There was not even any gun oil. You greased your rifle with olive oil, when you could get hold of it; at different times I have greased mine with vaseline, with cold cream, and even with bacon-fat. Moreover, there were no lanterns or electric torches – at this time there was not, I believe, such a thing as an electric torch throughout the whole of our sector of the front, and you could not buy one nearer than Barcelona, and only with difficulty even there.

As time went on, and the desultory rifle-fire rattled among the hills, I began to wonder with increasing scepticism whether anything would ever happen to bring a bit of life, or rather a bit of death, into this cock-eyed war. It was pneumonia that we were fighting against, not against men. When the trenches are more than five hundred yards apart no one gets hit except by accident. Of course there were casualties, but the majority of them were self-inflicted. If I remember rightly, the first five men I saw wounded in Spain were all wounded by our own weapons – I don't mean intentionally, but owing to accident or carelessness. Our worn-out rifles were a danger in themselves. Some of them had a nasty trick of going off if the butt was tapped on the ground; I saw a man shoot himself through the hand owing to this. And in the darkness the raw recruits were always firing at one another. One evening when it was barely even dusk a sentry let fly at me from a distance of twenty yards; but he missed me by a yard – goodness knows how many times the Spanish standard of marksmanship has saved my life. Another time I had gone out on patrol in the mist and had carefully warned the guard commander beforehand. But in coming back I stumbled against a bush, the startled sentry called out that the Fascists were coming, and I had the pleasure of hearing the guard commander order everyone to open rapid fire in my direction. Of course I lay down and the bullets went harmlessly over me. Nothing will convince a Spaniard, at least a young Spaniard, that fire-arms are dangerous. Once, rather later than this, I was photographing some machine-gunners with their gun, which was pointed directly towards me.

'Don't fire,' I said half-jokingly as I focused the camera.

'Oh no, we won't fire.'

The next moment there was a frightful roar and a stream of bullets tore past my face so close that my cheek was stung by grains of cordite. It was unintentional, but the machine-gunners considered it a great joke. Yet only a few days earlier they had seen a mule-driver accidentally shot by a political delegate who was playing the fool with an automatic pistol and had put five bullets in the mule-driver's lungs.

The difficult passwords which the army was using at this time were a minor source of danger. They were those tiresome double passwords in which one word has to be answered by another. Usually they were of an elevating and revolutionary nature, such as *Cultura – progresso*, or *Seremos – invencibles*, and it was often impossible to get illiterate sentries to remember these highfalutin' words; One night, I remember, the password was *Cataluña – heroica*, and a moon-faced peasant lad named Jaime Domenech approached me, greatly puzzled, and asked me to explain.

'*Heroica* – what does *heroica* mean?'

I told him that it meant the same as *valiente*. A little while later he was stumbling up the trench in the darkness, and the sentry challenged him:

'*Alto! Cataluña!*'

'*Valiente!*' yelled Jaime, certain that he was saying the right thing. Bang!

However, the sentry missed him. In this war everyone always did miss everyone else, when it was humanly possible.

IV

When I had been about three weeks in the line a contingent of twenty or thirty men, sent out from England by the ILP, arrived at Alcubierre, and in order to keep the English on this front together Williams and I were sent to join them. Our new position was at Monte Trazo, several miles further west and within sight of Saragossa.

The position was perched on a sort of razor-back of limestone with dug-outs driven horizontally into the cliff like sand-martins' nests. They went into the ground for prodigious distances, and inside they were pitch dark and so low that you could not even kneel in them, let alone stand. On the peaks to the left of us there were two more POUM positions, one of them an object of fascination to every man in the line, because there were three militiawomen there who did the cooking. These women were not exactly beautiful, but it was found necessary to put the position out of bounds to men of other companies. Five hundred yards to our right there was a PSUC post at the bend of the Alcubierre road. It was just here that the road changed hands. At night you could watch the lamps of our supply-lorries winding out from Alcubierre and, simultaneously, those of the Fascists coming from Saragossa. You could see Saragossa itself, a thin string of lights like the lighted port-holes of a ship, twelve miles south-westward. The Government troops had gazed at it from that distance since August 1936, and they are gazing at it still.

There were about thirty of ourselves, including one Spaniard (Ramón, Williams's brother-in-law), and there were a dozen Spanish machine-gunners. Apart from the one or two inevitable nuisances – for, as everyone knows, war attracts riff-raff – the English were an exceptionally good crowd, both physically and mentally. Perhaps the best of the bunch was Bob Smillie – the grandson of the famous miners' leader – who afterwards died such an evil and meaningless death in Valencia. It says a lot for the Spanish character that the English and the Spaniards always got on well together, in spite of the language difficulty. All Spaniards, we discovered, knew two English expressions. One was 'OK, baby,' the other was a word used by the Barcelona whores in their dealings with English sailors, and I am afraid the compositors would not print it.

Once again there was nothing happening all along the line: only the random crack of bullets and, very rarely, the crash of a Fascist mortar that sent everyone running to the top trench to see which hill the shells were bursting on. The enemy was somewhat closer to us here, perhaps three or four hundred yards away. Their nearest position was exactly opposite ours, with a machine-gun nest whose loopholes constantly tempted one to waste cartridges. The Fascists seldom bothered with rifle-shots, but sent bursts of accurate machine-gun fire at anyone who exposed himself. Nevertheless it was ten days or more before we had our first casualty.

The troops opposite us were Spaniards, but according to the deserters there were a few German NCOs among them. At some time in the past there had also been Moors there – poor devils, how they must have felt the cold – for out in no-man's-land there was a dead Moor who was one of the sights of the locality. A mile or two to the left of us the line ceased to be continuous and there was a tract of country, lower-lying and thickly wooded, which belonged neither to the Fascists nor ourselves. Both we and they used to make daylight patrols there. It was not bad fun in a Boy Scoutish way, though I never saw a Fascist patrol nearer than several hundred yards. By a lot of crawling on your belly you could work your way partly through the Fascist lines and could even see the farm-house flying the monarchist flag, which was the local Fascist head-quarters. Occasionally we gave it a rifle-volley and then slipped into cover before the machine-guns could locate us. I hope we broke a few windows, but it was a good eight hundred metres away, and with our rifles you could not make sure of hitting even a house at that range.

The weather was mostly clear and cold; sometimes sunny at midday, but always cold. Here and there in the soil of the hill-sides you found the green beaks of wild crocuses or irises poking through; evidently spring was coming, but coming very slowly. The nights were colder than ever. Coming off guard in the small hours we used to rake together what was left of the cook-house fire and then stand in the red-hot embers. It was bad for your boots, but it was very good for your feet.

But there were mornings when the sight of the dawn among the mountain-tops made it almost worthwhile to be out of bed at godless hours. I hate mountains, even from a spectacular point of view. But sometimes the dawn breaking behind the hill-tops in our rear, the first narrow streaks of gold, like swords slitting the darkness, and then the growing light and the seas of carmine cloud stretching away into inconceivable distances, were worth watching even when you had been up all night, when your legs were numb from the knees down and you were sullenly reflecting that there was no hope of food for another three hours. I saw the dawn more often during this campaign than during the rest of my life put together – or during the part that is to come, I hope.

We were short-handed here, which meant longer guards and more fatigues. I was beginning to suffer a little from the lack of sleep which is inevitable even in the quietest kind of war. Apart from guard-duties and patrols there were constant night-alarms and stand-to's, and in any case you can't sleep properly in a beastly hole in the ground with your feet aching with the cold. In my first three or four months in the line I do not suppose I had more than a dozen periods of twenty-four hours that were completely without sleep; on the other hand I certainly did not have a dozen nights of full sleep. Twenty or thirty hours' sleep in a week was quite a normal amount. The effects of this were not so bad as might be expected; one grew very stupid, and the job of climbing up and down the hills grew harder instead of easier, but one felt well and one was constantly hungry – heavens, how hungry! All food seemed good, even the eternal haricot beans which everyone in Spain finally learned to hate the sight of. Our water, what there was of it, came from miles away, on the backs of mules or little persecuted donkeys. For some reason the Aragón peasants treated their mules well but their donkeys abominably. If a donkey refused to go it was quite usual to kick him in the testicles. The issue of candles had ceased, and matches were running short. The Spaniards taught us how to make olive oil lamps out of a condensed milk tin, a cartridge-clip, and a bit of rag. When you had any olive oil, which was not often, these things would burn with a smoky flicker, about a quarter candle-power, just enough to find your rifle by.

There seemed no hope of any real fighting. When we left Monte Pocero I had counted my cartridges and found that in nearly three weeks I had fired just three shots at the enemy. They say it takes a thousand bullets to kill a man, and at this rate it would be twenty years before I killed my first Fascist. At Monte Trazo the lines were closer and one fired oftener, but I am reasonably certain that I never hit anyone. As a matter of fact, on this front and at this period of the war the real weapon was not the rifle but the megaphone. Being unable to kill your enemy you shouted at him instead. This method of warfare is so extraordinary that it needs explaining.

Wherever the lines were within hailing distance of one another there was always a good deal of shouting from trench to trench. From ourselves *'Fascistas –*

maricones!' From the Fascists: '*Viva España! Viva Franco!*' – or, when they knew that there were English opposite them: 'Go home, you English! We don't want foreigners here!' On the Government side, in the party militias, the shouting of propaganda to undermine the enemy morale had been developed into a regular technique. In every suitable position men, usually machine-gunners, were told off for shouting-duty and provided with megaphones. Generally they shouted a set-piece, full of revolutionary sentiments which explained to the Fascist soldiers that they were merely the hirelings of international capitalism, that they were fighting against their own class, etc. etc., and urged them to come over to our side. This was repeated over and over by relays of men; sometimes it continued almost the whole night. There is very little doubt that it had its effect, everyone agreed that the trickle of Fascist deserters was partly caused by it. If one comes to think of it, when some poor devil of a sentry – very likely a Socialist or Anarchist trade union member who has been conscripted against his will – is freezing at his post, the slogan 'Don't fight against your own class!' ringing again and again through the darkness is bound to make an impression on him. It might make just the difference between deserting and not deserting. Of course such a proceeding does not fit in with the English conception of war. I admit I was amazed and scandalized when I first saw it done. The idea of trying to convert your enemy instead of shooting him! I now think that from any point of view it was a legitimate manoeuvre. In ordinary trench warfare, when there is no artillery, it is extremely difficult to inflict casualties on the enemy without receiving an equal number yourself. If you can immobilize a certain number of men by making them desert, so much the better; deserters are actually more useful to you than corpses, because they can give information. But at the beginning it dismayed all of us; it made us feel that the Spaniards were not taking this war of theirs sufficiently seriously. The man who did the shouting at the PSUC post down on our right was an artist at the job. Sometimes, instead of shouting revolutionary slogans he simply told the Fascists how much better we were fed than they were. His account of the Government rations was apt to be a little imaginative. 'Buttered toast!' – you could hear his voice echoing across the lonely valley – 'We're just sitting down to buttered toast over here. Lovely slices of buttered toast!' I do not doubt that, like the rest of us, he had not seen butter for weeks or months past, but in the icy night the news of buttered toast probably set many a Fascist mouth watering. It even made mine water, though I knew he was lying.

One day in February we saw a Fascist aeroplane approaching. As usual, a machine-gun was dragged into the open and its barrel cocked up, and everyone lay on his back to get a good aim. Our isolated positions were not worth bombing, and as a rule the few Fascist aeroplanes that passed our way circled round to avoid machine-gun fire. This time the aeroplane came straight over, too high up to be worth shooting at, and out of it came tumbling not bombs but white glittering things that turned over and over in the air. A few fluttered down into the position. They were copies of a Fascist newspaper, the *Heraldo de Aragón*, announcing the fall of Málaga.

That night the Fascists made a sort of abortive attack. I was just getting down into kip, half dead with sleep, when there was a heavy stream of bullets overhead and someone shouted into the dug-out: 'They're attacking!' I grabbed my rifle and slithered up to my post, which was at the top of the position, beside the machine-gun. There was utter darkness and diabolical noise. The fire of, I think, five machine-guns was pouring upon us, and there was a series of heavy crashes caused by the Fascists flinging bombs over their own parapet in the most idiotic manner. It was intensely dark. Down in the valley to the left of us I could see the greenish flash of rifles where a small party of Fascists, probably a patrol, were chipping in. The bullets were flying round us in the darkness, crack-zip-crack. A few shells came whistling over, but they fell nowhere near us and (as usual in this war) most of them failed to explode. I had a bad moment when yet another machine-gun opened fire from the hill-top in our rear – actually a gun that had been brought up to support us, but at the time it looked as though we were surrounded. Presently our own machine-gun jammed, as it always did jam with those vile cartridges, and the ramrod was lost in the impenetrable darkness. Apparently there was nothing that one could do except stand still and be shot at. The Spanish machine-gunners disdained to take cover, in fact exposed themselves deliberately, so I had to do likewise. Petty though it was, the whole experience was very interesting. It was the first time that I had been properly speaking under fire, and to my humiliation I found that I was horribly frightened. You always, I notice, feel the same when you are under heavy fire – not so much afraid of being hit as afraid because you don't know *where* you will be hit. You are wondering all the while just where the bullet will nip you, and it gives your whole body a most unpleasant sensitiveness.

After an hour or two the firing slowed down and died away. Meanwhile we had had only one casualty. The Fascists had advanced a couple of machine-guns into no-man's-land, but they had kept at a safe distance and made no attempt to storm our parapet. They were in fact not attacking, merely wasting cartridges and making a cheerful noise to celebrate the fall of Málaga. The chief importance of the affair was that it taught me to read the war news in the papers with a more disbelieving eye. A day or two later the newspapers and the radio published reports of a tremendous attack with cavalry and tanks (up a perpendicular hill-side!) which had been beaten off by the heroic English.

When the Fascists told us that Málaga had fallen we set it down as a lie, but next day there were more convincing rumours, and it must have been a day or two later that it was admitted officially. By degrees the whole disgraceful story leaked out – how the town had been evacuated without firing a shot, and how the fury of the Italians had fallen not upon the troops, who were gone, but upon the wretched civilian population, some of whom were pursued and machine-gunned for a hundred miles. The news sent a sort of chill all along the line, for, whatever the truth may have been, every man in the militia believed that the loss of Málaga was due to treachery. It was the first talk I had heard of treachery or divided aims. It set up in my mind the first vague doubt about this war in which, hitherto, the rights and wrongs had seemed so beautifully simple.

In mid-February we left Monte Trazo and were sent, together with all the POUM troops in this sector, to make a part of the army besieging Huesca. It was a fifty-mile lorry journey across the wintry plain, where the clipped vines were not yet budding and the blades of the winter barley were just poking through the lumpy soil. Four kilometres from our new trenches Huesca glittered small and clear like a city of dolls' houses. Months earlier, when Siétamo was taken, the general commanding the Government troops had said gaily: 'Tomorrow we'll have coffee in Huesca.' It turned out that he was mistaken. There had been bloody attacks, but the town did not fall, and 'Tomorrow we'll have coffee in Huesca' had become a standing joke throughout the army. If I ever go back to Spain I shall make a point of having a cup of coffee in Huesca.

V

On the eastern side of Huesca, until late March, nothing happened – almost literally nothing. We were twelve hundred metres from the enemy. When the Fascists were driven back into Huesca the Republican

Army troops who held this part of the line had not been over-zealous in their advance, so that the line formed a kind of pocket. Later it would have to be advanced – a ticklish job under fire – but for the present the enemy might as well have been non-existent; our sole preoccupation was keeping warm and getting enough to eat.

Meanwhile, the daily – more particularly nightly – round, the common task. Sentry-go, patrols, digging; mud, rain, shrieking winds, and occasional snow. It was not till well into April that the nights grew noticeably warmer. Up here on the plateau the March days were mostly like an English March, with bright blue skies and nagging winds. The winter barley was a foot high, crimson buds were forming on the cherry trees (the line here ran through deserted orchards and vegetable gardens), and if you searched the ditches you could find violets and a kind of wild hyacinth like a poor specimen of a bluebell. Immediately behind the line there ran a wonderful, green, bubbling stream, the first transparent water I had seen since coming to the front. One day I set my teeth and crawled into the river to have my first bath in six weeks. It was what you might call a brief bath, for the water was mainly snow-water and not much above freezing-point.

Meanwhile nothing happened, nothing ever happened. The English had got into the habit of saying that this wasn't a war, it was a bloody pantomime. We were hardly under direct fire from the Fascists. The only danger was from stray bullets, which, as the lines curved forward on either side, came from several directions. All the casualties at this time were from strays. Arthur Clinton got a mysterious bullet that smashed his left shoulder and disabled his arm, permanently, I am afraid. There was a little shell-fire, but it was extraordinarily ineffectual. The scream and crash of the shells was actually looked upon as a mild diversion. The Fascists never dropped their shells on our parapet. A few hundred yards behind us there was a country house, called La Granja, with big farm-buildings, which was used as a store, headquarters, and cook-house for this sector of the line. It was this that the Fascist gunners were trying for, but they were five or six kilometres away and they never aimed well enough to do more than smash the windows and chip the walls. You were only in danger if you happened to be coming up the road when the firing started, and the shells plunged into the fields on either side of you. One learned almost immediately the mysterious art of knowing by the sound of a shell how close it will fall. The shells the Fascists were firing at this period were wretchedly bad. Although they were 150 mm they only made a crater about six feet wide by four deep, and at least one in four failed to explode. There were the usual romantic tales of sabotage in the Fascist factories and unexploded shells in which, instead of the charge, there was found a scrap of paper saying 'Red Front', but I never saw one. The truth was that the shells were hopelessly old; someone picked up a brass fuse-cap stamped with the date, and it was 1917. The Fascist guns were of the same make and calibre as our own, and the unexploded shells were often reconditioned and fired back. There was said to be one old shell with a nickname of its own which travelled daily to and fro, never exploding.

At night small patrols used to be sent into no-man's-land to lie in ditches near the Fascist lines and listen for sounds (bugle-calls, motor-horns, and so forth) that indicated activity in Huesca. There was a constant come-and-go of Fascist troops, and the numbers could be checked to some extent from listeners' reports. We always had special orders to report the ringing of church bells. It seemed that the Fascists always heard mass before going into action. In among the fields and orchards there were deserted mud-walled huts which it was safe to explore with a lighted match when you had plugged up the windows. Sometimes you came on valuable pieces of loot such as a hatchet or a Fascist water-bottle (better than ours and greatly sought after). You could explore in the daytime as well, but mostly it had to be done crawling on all fours. It was queer to creep about in those empty, fertile fields where everything had been arrested just at the harvest-moment. Last year's crops had never been touched. The unpruned vines were snaking across the ground, the cobs on the standing maize had gone as hard as stone, the mangels and sugar-beets were hypertrophied into huge woody lumps. How the peasants must have cursed both armies! Sometimes parties of men went spud-gathering in no-man's-land. About a mile to the right of us, where the lines were closer together, there was a patch of potatoes that was frequented both by the Fascists and ourselves. We went there in the daytime, they only at night, as it was commanded by our machine-guns. One night to our annoyance they turned out *en masse* and cleared up the whole patch. We discovered another patch further on, where there was practically no cover and you had to lift the potatoes lying on your belly – a fatiguing job. If their machine-gunners spotted you, you had to flatten yourself out like a rat when it squirms under a door, with the bullets cutting up the clods a few yards behind you. It seemed worth it at the time. Potatoes were getting very scarce. If you got a sackful you could take them down to the cook-house and swap them for a water-bottleful of coffee.

And still nothing happened, nothing ever looked like happening. 'When are we going to attack? Why don't we attack?' were the questions you heard night and day from Spaniard and Englishman alike. When you think what fighting means it is queer that soldiers want to fight, and yet undoubtedly they do. In stationary warfare there are three things that all soldiers long for: a battle, more cigarettes, and a week's leave. We were somewhat better armed now than before. Each man had a hundred and fifty rounds of ammunition instead of fifty, and by degrees we were being issued with bayonets, steel helmets, and a few bombs. There were constant rumours of forthcoming battles, which I have since thought were deliberately circulated to keep up the spirits of the troops. It did not need much military knowledge to see that there would be no major action on this side of Huesca, at any rate for the time being. The strategic point was the road to Jaca, over on the other side. Later, when the Anarchists made their attacks on the Jaca road, our job was to make 'holding attacks' and force the Fascists to divert troops from the other side.

During all this time, about six weeks, there was only one action on our part of the front. This was when our Shock Troopers attacked the Manicomio, a disused lunatic asylum which the Fascists had converted into a fortress. There were several hundred refugee Germans serving with the POUM. They were organized in a special battalion called the Battallon de Choque, and from a military point of view they were on quite a different level from the rest of the militia – indeed, were more like soldiers than anyone I saw in Spain, except the Assault Guards and some of the International Column. The attack was mucked up, as usual. How many operations in this war, on the Government side, were *not* mucked up, I wonder? The Shock Troops took the Manicomio by storm, but the troops, of I forget which militia, who were to support them by seizing the neighbouring hill that commanded the Manicomio, were badly let down. The captain who led them was one of those Regular Army officers of doubtful loyalty whom the Government persisted in employing. Either from fright or treachery he warned the Fascists by flinging a bomb when they were two hundred yards away. I am glad to say his men shot him dead on the spot. But the surprise-attack was no surprise, and the militiamen were mown down by heavy fire and driven off the hill, and at nightfall the Shock Troops had to abandon the Manicomio. Through the night the ambulances filed down the abominable road to Siétamo, killing the badly wounded with their joltings.

All of us were lousy by this time; though still cold it was warm enough for that. I have had a big experience of body vermin of various kinds, and for sheer beastliness the louse beats everything I have encountered. Other insects, mosquitoes for instance, make you suffer more, but at least they aren't *resident* vermin. The human louse somewhat resembles a tiny lobster, and he lives chiefly in your trousers. Short of burning all your clothes there is no known way of getting rid of him. Down the seams of your trousers he lays his glittering white eggs, like tiny grains of rice, which hatch out and breed families of their own at horrible speed. I think the pacifists might find it helpful to illustrate their pamphlets with enlarged photographs of lice. Glory of war, indeed! In war *all* soldiers are lousy, at least when it is warm enough. The men who fought at Verdun, at Waterloo, at Flodden, at Senlac, at Thermopylae – every one of them had lice crawling over his testicles. We kept the brutes down to some extent by burning out the eggs and by bathing as often as we could face it. Nothing short of lice could have driven me into that ice-cold river.

Everything was running short – boots, clothes, tobacco, soap, candles, matches, olive oil. Our uniforms were dropping to pieces, and many of the men had no boots, only rope-soled sandals. You came on piles of worn-out boots everywhere. Once we kept a dug-out fire burning for two days mainly with boots, which are not bad fuel. By this time my wife was in Barcelona and used to send me tea, chocolate, and even cigars when such things were procurable; but even in Barcelona everything was running short, especially tobacco. The tea was a godsend, though we had no milk and seldom any sugar. Parcels were constantly being sent from England to men in the contingent, but they never arrived; food, clothes, cigarettes – everything was either refused by the Post Office or seized in France. Curiously enough, the only firm that succeeded in sending packets of tea – even, on one memorable occasion, a tin of biscuits – to my wife was the Army and Navy Stores. Poor old Army and Navy! They did their duty nobly, but perhaps they might have felt happier if the stuff had been going to Franco's side of the barricade. The shortage of tobacco was the worst of all. At the beginning we had been issued with a packet of cigarettes a day, then it got down to eight cigarettes a day, then to five. Finally there were ten deadly days when there was no issue of tobacco at all. For the first time, in Spain, I saw something that you see every day in London – people picking up fag-ends.

Towards the end of March I got a poisoned hand that had to be lanced and put in a sling. I had to go into hospital, but it was not worth sending me to Siétamo for such a petty injury, so I stayed in the so-called hospital at Monflorite, which was merely a casualty clearing station. I was there ten days, part of the time in bed. The *practicantes* (hospital assistants) stole practically every valuable object I possessed, including my camera and all my photographs. At the front everyone stole, it was the inevitable effect of shortage, but the hospital people were always the worst. Later, in the hospital at Barcelona, an American who had come to join the International Column on a ship that was torpedoed by an Italian submarine, told me how he was carried ashore wounded, and how, even as they lifted him into the ambulance, the stretcher-bearers pinched his wrist-watch.

While my arm was in the sling I spent several blissful days wandering about the countryside. Monflorite was the usual huddle of mud and stone houses, with narrow tortuous alleys that had been churned by lorries till they looked like the craters of the moon. The church had been badly knocked about but was used as a military store. In the whole neighbourhood there were only two farmhouses of any size, Torre Lorenzo and Torre Fabián, and only two really large buildings, obviously the houses of the landowners who had once lorded it over the countryside; you could see their wealth reflected in the miserable huts of the peasants. Just behind the river, close to the front line, there was an enormous flour mill with a country house attached to it. It seemed shameful to see the huge costly machines rusting useless and the wooden flour-chutes torn down for firewood. Later on, to get firewood for the troops further back, parties of men were sent in lorries to wreck the place systematically. They used to smash the floorboards of a room by bursting a handgrenade in it. La Granja, our store and cookhouse, had possibly at one time been a convent. It had huge courtyards and outhouses, covering an acre or more, with stabling for thirty or forty horses. The country houses in that part of Spain are of no interest architecturally, but their farm-buildings, of lime-washed stone with round arches and magnificent roof-beams, are noble places, built on a plan that has probably not altered for centuries. Sometimes it gave you a sneaking sympathy with the Fascist ex-owners to see the way the militia treated the buildings they had seized. In La Granja every room that was not in use had been turned into a latrine – a frightful shambles of smashed furniture and excrement. The little church that adjoined it, its walls perforated by shell-holes, had its floor inches deep in dung. In the great courtyard where the cooks ladled out the rations, the litter of rusty tins, mud, mule dung, and decaying food was revolting. It gave point to the old army song:

> *There are rats, rats,*
> *Rats as big as cats,*
> *In the quartermaster's store!*

The ones at La Granja itself really were as big as cats, or nearly; great bloated brutes that waddled over the beds of muck, too impudent even to run away unless you shot at them.

Spring was really here at last. The blue in the sky was softer, the air grew suddenly balmy. The frogs were mating noisily in the ditches. Round the drinking-pool that served for the village mules I found exquisite green frogs the size of a penny, so brilliant that the young grass looked dull beside them. Peasant lads went out with buckets hunting for snails, which they roasted alive on sheets of tin. As soon as the weather improved the peasants had turned out for the spring ploughing. It is typical of the utter vagueness in which the Spanish agrarian revolution is wrapped that I could not even discover for certain whether the land here was collectivized or whether the peasants had simply divided it up among themselves. I fancy that in theory it was collectivized, this being POUM and Anarchist territory. At any rate the landowners were gone, the fields were being cultivated, and people seemed satisfied. The friendliness of the peasants towards ourselves never ceased to astonish me. To some of the older ones the war must have seemed meaningless, visibly it produced a shortage of everything and a dismal dull life for everybody, and at the best of times peasants hate having troops quartered upon them. Yet they were invariably friendly – I suppose reflecting that, however intolerable we might be in other ways, we did stand between them and their one-time landlords. Civil war is a queer thing. Huesca was not five miles away, it was these people's market town, all of them had relatives there, every week of their lives they had gone there to sell their poultry and vegetables. And now for eight months an impenetrable barrier of barbed wire and machine-guns had lain between. Occasionally it slipped their memory. Once I was talking to an old woman who was carrying one of those tiny iron lamps in which the Spaniards burn olive oil. 'Where can I buy a lamp like that?' I said. 'In Huesca,' she said without thinking, and then we both laughed. The village girls were splendid vivid creatures with coal-black hair, a swinging walk, and a straightforward, man-to-man demeanour which was probably a by-product of the revolution.

Men in ragged blue shirts and black corduroy breeches, with broad-brimmed straw hats, were ploughing the fields behind teams of mules with rhythmically flopping ears. Their ploughs were wretched things, only stirring the soil, not cutting anything we should regard as a furrow. All the agricultural implements were pitifully antiquated, everything being governed by the expensiveness of metal. A broken ploughshare, for instance, was patched, and then patched again, till sometimes it was mainly patches. Rakes and pitchforks were made of wood. Spades, among a people who seldom possessed boots, were unknown: they did their digging with a clumsy hoe like those used in India. There was a kind of harrow that took one straight back to the later Stone Age. It was made of boards joined together, to about the size of a kitchen table; in the boards hundreds of holes were morticed, and into each hole was jammed a piece of flint which had been chipped into shape exactly as men used to chip them ten thousand years ago. I remember my feeling almost of horror when I first came upon one of these things in a derelict hut in no-man's-land. I had to puzzle over it for a long while before grasping that it was a harrow. It made me sick to think of the work that must go into the making of such a thing, and the poverty that was obliged to use flint in place of steel. I have felt more kindly towards industrializm ever since. But in the village there were two up-to-date farm tractors, no doubt seized from some big landowner's estate.

Once or twice I wandered out to the little walled graveyard that stood a mile or so from the village. The dead from the front were normally sent to Siétamo; these were the village dead. It was queerly different from an English graveyard. No reverence for the dead here! Everything overgrown with bushes and coarse grass, human bones littered everywhere. But the really surprising thing was the almost complete lack of religious inscriptions on the gravestones, though they all dated from before the revolution. Only once, I think, I saw the 'Pray for the soul of so-and-so' which is usual on Catholic graves. Most of the inscriptions were purely secular, with ludicrous poems about the virtues of the deceased. On perhaps one grave in four or five there was a small cross or a perfunctory reference to Heaven; this had usually been chipped off by some industrious atheist with a chisel.

It struck me that the people in this part of Spain must be genuinely without religious feeling – religious feeling, I mean, in the orthodox sense. It is curious that all the time I was in Spain I never once saw a person cross himself; yet you would think such a movement would become instinctive, revolution or no revolution. Obviously the Spanish Church will come back (as the saying goes, night and the Jesuits always return) but there is no doubt that at the outbreak of the revolution it collapsed and was smashed up to an extent that would be unthinkable even for the moribund C of E in like circumstances. To the Spanish people, at any rate in Catalonia and Aragón, the Church was a racket pure and simple. And possibly Christian belief was replaced to some extent by Anarchism, whose influence is widely spread and which undoubtedly has a religious tinge.

It was the day I came back from hospital that we advanced the line to what was really its proper position, about a thousand yards forward, along the little stream that lay a couple of hundred yards in front of the Fascist line. This operation ought to have been carried out months earlier. The point of doing it now was that the Anarchists were attacking on the Jaca road, and to advance on this side made them divert troops to face us.

We were sixty or seventy hours without sleep, and my memories go down into a sort of blur, or rather a series of pictures. Listening-duty in no-man's-land, a hundred yards from the Casa Francesa, a fortified farmhouse which was part of the Fascist line. Seven hours lying in a horrible marsh, in reedy-smelling water into which one's body subsided gradually deeper and deeper: the reedy smell, the numbing cold, the stars immovable in the black sky, the harsh croaking of the frogs. Though this was April it was the coldest night that I remember in Spain. Only a hundred yards behind us the working-parties were hard at it, but there was utter silence except for the chorus of the frogs. Just once during the night I heard a sound – the familiar noise of a sandbag being flattened with a spade. It is queer how, just now and again, Spaniards can carry out a brilliant feat of organization. The whole move was beautifully planned. In seven hours six hundred men constructed twelve hundred metres of trench and parapet, at distances of from a hundred and fifty to three hundred yards from the Fascist line, and all so silently that the Fascists heard nothing, and during the night there was only one casualty. There were more next day, of course. Every man had his job assigned to him, even to the cook-house orderlies who suddenly arrived when the work was done with buckets of wine laced with brandy.

And then the dawn coming up and the Fascists suddenly discovering that we were there. The square white block of the Casa Francesa, though it was two hundred yards away, seemed to tower over us, and the machine-guns in its sand-bagged upper windows seemed to be pointing straight down into the trench. We all stood gaping at it, wondering why the Fascists didn't see us. Then a vicious swirl of bullets, and everyone had flung himself on his knees and was frantically digging, deepening the trench and scooping out small shelters in the side. My arm was still in bandages, I could not dig, and I spent most of that day reading a detective story – *The Missing Moneylender* its name was. I don't remember the plot of it, but I remember very clearly the feeling of sitting there reading it; the dampish clay of the trench bottom underneath me, the constant shifting of my legs out of the way as men hurried stooping down the trench, the crack-crack-crack of bullets a foot or two overhead. Thomas Parker got a bullet through the top of his thigh, which, as he said, was nearer to being a DSO[3] than he cared about.

[3] Dickie shot off.

Casualties were happening all along the line, but nothing to what there would have been if they had caught us on the move during the night. A deserter told us afterwards that five Fascist sentries were shot for negligence. Even now they could have massacred us if they had had the initiative to bring up a few mortars. It was an awkward job getting the wounded down the narrow, crowded trench. I saw one poor devil, his breeches dark with blood, flung out of his stretcher and gasping in agony. One had to carry wounded men a long distance, a mile or more, for even when a road existed the ambulances never came very near the front line. If they came too near the Fascists had a habit of shelling them – justifiably, for in modern war no one scruples to use an ambulance for carrying ammunition.

And then, next night, waiting at Torre Fabián for an attack that was called off at the last moment by wireless. In the barn where we waited the floor was a thin layer of chaff over deep beds of bones, human bones and cows' bones mixed up, and the place was alive with rats. The filthy brutes came swarming out of the ground on every side. If there is one thing I hate more than another it is a rat running over me in the darkness. However, I had the satisfaction of catching one of them a good punch that sent him flying.

And then waiting fifty or sixty yards from the Fascist parapet for the order to attack. A long line of men crouching in an irrigation ditch with their bayonets peeping over the edge and the whites of their eyes shining through the darkness. Kopp and Benjamin squatting behind us with a man who had a wireless receiving-box strapped to his shoulders. On the western horizon rosy gun-flashes followed at intervals of several seconds by enormous explosions. And then a pip-pip-pip noise from the wireless and the whispered order that we were to get out of it while the going was good. We did so, but not quickly enough. Twelve wretched children of the JCI (the Youth League of the POUM, corresponding to the JSU of the PSUC) who had been posted only about forty yards from the Fascist parapet, were caught by the dawn and unable to escape. All day they had to lie there, with only tufts of grass for cover, the Fascists shooting at them every time they moved. By nightfall seven were dead, then the other five managed to creep away in the darkness.

And then, for many mornings to follow, the sound of the Anarchist attacks on the other side of Huesca. Always the same sound. Suddenly, at some time in the small hours, the opening crash of several score bombs bursting simultaneously – even from miles away a diabolical, rending crash – and then the unbroken roar of massed rifles and machine-guns, a heavy rolling sound curiously similar to the roll of drums. By degrees the firing would spread all round the lines that encircled Huesca, and we would stumble out into the trench to lean sleepily against the parapet while a ragged meaningless fire swept overhead.

In the daytime the guns thundered fitfully. Torre Fabián, now our cookhouse, was shelled and partially destroyed. It is curious that when you are watching artillery-fire from a safe distance you always want the gunner to hit his mark, even though the mark contains your dinner and some of your comrades. The Fascists were shooting well that morning; perhaps there were German gunners on the job. They bracketed neatly on Torre Fabián. One shell beyond it, one shell short of it, then whizz-BOOM! Burst rafters leaping upwards and a sheet of uralite skimming down the air like a flicked playing card. The next shell took off the corner of a building as neatly as a giant might do it with a knife. But the cooks produced dinner on time – a memorable feat.

As the days went on the unseen but audible guns began each to assume a distinct personality. There were the two batteries of Russian 75-mm guns which fired from close in our rear and which somehow evoked in my mind the picture of a fat man hitting a golf ball. These were the first Russian guns I had seen – or heard, rather. They had a low trajectory and a very high velocity, so that you heard the cartridge explosion, the whizz and the shell-burst almost simultaneously. Behind Monflorite were two very heavy guns which fired a few times a day, with a deep, muffled roar that was like the baying of distant chained-up monsters. Up at Mount Aragón, the medieval fortress which the Government troops had stormed last year (the first time in its history, it was said), and which guarded one of the approaches to Huesca, there was a heavy gun which must have dated well back into the nineteenth century. Its great shells whistled over so slowly that you felt certain you could run beside them and keep up with them. A shell from this gun sounded like nothing so much as a man riding along on a bicycle and whistling. The trench-mortars, small though they were, made the most evil sound of all. Their shells are really a kind of winged torpedo, shaped like the darts thrown in public houses and about the size of a quart bottle; they go off with a devilish metallic crash, as of some monstrous globe of brittle steel being shattered on an anvil. Sometimes our aeroplanes flew over and let loose the aerial torpedoes whose tremendous echoing roar makes the earth tremble even at two miles' distance. The shell-bursts from the Fascist anti-aircraft guns dotted the sky like cloudlets in a bad watercolour, but I never saw them get within a thousand yards of an aeroplane. When an aeroplane swoops down and uses its machine-gun the sound, from below, is like the fluttering of wings.

On our part of the line not much was happening. Two hundred yards to the right of us, where the Fascists were on higher ground, their snipers picked off a few of our comrades. Two hundred yards to the left, at the bridge over the stream, a sort of duel was going on between the Fascist mortars and the men who were building a concrete barricade across the bridge. The evil little shells whizzed over, zwing-crash! zwing-crash!, making a doubly diabolical noise when they landed on the asphalt road. A hundred yards away you could stand in perfect safety and watch the columns of earth and black smoke leaping into the air like magic trees. The poor devils round the bridge spent much of the daytime cowering in the little manholes they had scooped in the side of the trench. But there were less casualties than might have been expected, and the barricade rose steadily, a wall of concrete two feet thick with embrasures for two machine-guns and a small field-gun. The concrete was being reinforced with old bedsteads, which apparently was the only iron that could be found for the purpose.

VI

One afternoon Benjamin told us that he wanted fifteen volunteers. The attack on the Fascist redoubt which had been called off on the previous occasion was to be carried out tonight. I oiled my ten Mexican cartridges, dirtied my bayonet (the things give your position away if they flash too much), and packed up a hunk of bread, three inches of red sausage, and a cigar which my wife had sent from Barcelona and which I had been hoarding for a long time. Bombs were served out, three to a man. The Spanish Government had at last succeeded in producing a decent bomb. It was on the principle of a Mills bomb, but with two pins instead of one. After you had pulled the pins out there was an interval of seven seconds before the bomb exploded. Its chief disadvantage was that one pin was very stiff and the other very loose, so that you had the choice of leaving both pins in place and being unable to pull the stiff one out in a moment of emergency, or pulling out the stiff one beforehand and being in a constant stew lest the thing should explode in your pocket. But it was a handy little bomb to throw.

A little before midnight Benjamin led the fifteen of

us down to Torre Fabián. Ever since evening the rain had been pelting down. The irrigation ditches were brimming over, and every time you stumbled into one you were in water up to your waist. In the pitch darkness and sheeting rain in the farmyard a dim mass of men was waiting. Kopp addressed us, first in Spanish, then in English, and explained the plan of attack. The Fascist line here made an L-bend and the parapet we were to attack lay on rising ground at the corner of the L. About thirty of us, half English and half Spanish, under the command of Jorge Roca, our battalion commander (a battalion in the militia was about four hundred men), and Benjamin, were to creep up and cut the Fascist wire. Jorge would fling the first bomb as a signal, then the rest of us were to send in a rain of bombs, drive the Fascists out of the parapet and seize it before they could rally. Simultaneously seventy Shock Troopers were to assault the next Fascist 'position', which lay two hundred yards to the right of the other, joined to it by a communication-trench. To prevent us from shooting each other in the darkness white armlets would be worn. At this moment a messenger arrived to say that there were no white armlets. Out of the darkness a plaintive voice suggested: 'Couldn't we arrange for the Fascists to wear white armlets instead?'

There was an hour or two to put in. The barn over the mule stable was so wrecked by shell-fire that you could not move about in it without a light. Half the floor had been torn away by a plunging shell and there was a twenty-foot drop onto the stones beneath. Someone found a pick and levered a burst plank out of the floor, and in a few minutes we had got a fire alight and our drenched clothes were steaming. Someone else produced a pack of cards. A rumour – one of those mysterious rumours that are endemic in war – flew round that hot coffee with brandy in it was about to be served out. We filed eagerly down the almost-collapsing staircase and wandered round the dark yard, enquiring where the coffee was to be found. Alas! there was no coffee. Instead, they called us together, ranged us into single file, and then Jorge and Benjamin set off rapidly into the darkness, the rest of us following.

It was still raining and intensely dark, but the wind had dropped. The mud was unspeakable. The paths through the beet-fields were simply a succession of lumps, as slippery as a greasy pole, with huge pools everywhere. Long before we got to the place where we were to leave our own parapet everyone had fallen several times and our rifles were coated with mud. At the parapet a small knot of men, our reserves, were waiting, and the doctor and a row of stretchers. We filed through the gap in the parapet and waded through another irrigation ditch. Splash-gurgle! Once again in water up to your waist, with the filthy, slimy mud oozing over your boot-tops. On the grass outside Jorge waited till we were all through. Then, bent almost double, he began creeping slowly forward. The Fascist parapet was about a hundred and fifty yards away. Our one chance of getting there was to move without noise.

I was in front with Jorge and Benjamin. Bent double, but with faces raised, we crept into the almost utter darkness at a pace that grew slower at every step. The rain beat lightly in our faces. When I glanced back I could see the men who were nearest to me, a bunch of humped shapes like huge black mushrooms gliding slowly forward. But every time I raised my head Benjamin, close beside me, whispered fiercely in my ear: 'To keep ze head down! To keep ze head down!' I could have told him that he needn't worry. I knew by experiment that on a dark night you can never see a man at twenty paces. It was far more important to go quietly. If they once heard us we were done for. They had only to spray the darkness with their machine-gun and there was nothing for it but to run or be massacred.

But on the sodden ground it was almost impossible to move quietly. Do what you would your feet stuck to the mud, and every step you took was slop-slop, slop-slop. And the devil of it was that the wind had dropped, and in spite of the rain it was a very quiet night. Sounds would carry a long way. There was a dreadful moment when I kicked against a tin and thought every Fascist within miles must have heard it. But no, not a sound, no answering shot, no movement in the Fascist lines. We crept onwards, always more slowly. I cannot convey to you the depth of my desire to get there. Just to get within bombing distance before they heard us! At such a time you have not even any fear, only a tremendous hopeless longing to get over the intervening ground. I have felt exactly the same thing when stalking a wild animal; the same agonized desire to get within range, the same dreamlike certainty that it is impossible. And how the distance stretched out! I knew the ground well, it was barely a hundred and fifty yards, and yet it seemed more like a mile. When you are creeping at that pace you are aware as an ant might be of the enormous variations in the ground; the splendid patch of smooth grass here, the evil patch of sticky mud there, the tall rustling reeds that have got to be avoided, the heap of stones that almost makes you give up hope because it seems impossible to get over it without noise.

We had been creeping forward for such an age that I began to think we had gone the wrong way. Then in the darkness thin parallel lines of something blacker were faintly visible. It was the outer wire (the Fascists had two lines of wire). Jorge knelt down, fumbled in his pocket. He had our only pair of wire-cutters. Snip, snip. The trailing stuff was lifted delicately aside. We waited for the men at the back to close up. They seemed to be making a frightful noise. It might be fifty yards to the Fascist parapet now. Still onwards, bent double. A stealthy step, lowering your foot as gently as a cat approaching a mousehole; then a pause to listen; then another step. Once I raised my head; in silence Benjamin put his hand behind my neck and pulled it violently down. I knew that the inner wire was barely twenty yards from the parapet. It seemed to me inconceivable that thirty men could get there unheard. Our breathing was enough to give us away. Yet somehow we did get there. The Fascist parapet was visible now, a dim black mound, looming high above us. Once again Jorge knelt and fumbled. Snip, snip. There was no way of cutting the stuff silently.

So that was the inner wire. We crawled through it

75

on all fours and rather more rapidly. If we had time to
deploy now all was well. Jorge and Benjamin crawled
across to the right. But the men behind, who were
spread out, had to form into single file to get through
the narrow gap in the wire, and just at this moment
there was a flash and a bang from the Fascist parapet.
The sentry had heard us at last. Jorge poised himself
on one knee and swung his arm like a bowler. Crash!
His bomb burst somewhere over the parapet. At once,
far more promptly than one would have thought possible, a roar of fire, ten or twenty rifles, burst out from
the Fascist parapet. They had been waiting for us after
all. Momentarily you could see every sandbag in the
lurid light. Men too far back were flinging their bombs
and some of them were falling short of the parapet.
Every loophole seemed to be spouting jets of flame. It
is always hateful to be shot at in the dark – every
rifle-flash seems to be pointed straight at yourself – but
it was the bombs that were the worst. You cannot
conceive the horror of these things till you have seen
one burst close to you and in darkness; in the daytime
there is only the crash of the explosion, in the darkness
there is the blinding red glare as well. I had flung
myself down at the first volley. All this while I was
lying on my side in the greasy mud wrestling savagely
with the pin of a bomb. The damned thing *would* not
come out. Finally I realized that I was twisting it in the
wrong direction. I got the pin out, rose to my knees,
hurled the bomb, and threw myself down again. The
bomb burst over to the right, outside the parapet: fright
had spoiled my aim. Just at this moment another bomb

burst right in front of me, so close that I could feel the heat of the explosion. I flattened myself out and dug my face into the mud so hard that I hurt my neck and thought that I was wounded. Through the din I heard an English voice behind me say quietly: 'I'm hit.' The bomb had, in fact, wounded several people round about me without touching myself. I rose to my knees and flung my second bomb. I forget where that one went.

The Fascists were firing, our people behind were firing, and I was very conscious of being in the middle. I felt the blast of a shot and realized that a man was firing from immediately behind me. I stood up and shouted at him: 'Don't shoot at me, you bloody fool!' At this moment I saw that Benjamin, ten or fifteen yards to my right, was motioning to me with his arm. I ran across to him. It meant crossing the line of spouting loop-holes, and as I went I clapped my left hand over my cheek; an idiotic gesture – as though one's hand could stop a bullet! – but I had a horror of being hit in the face. Benjamin was kneeling on one knee with a pleased, devilish sort of expression on his face and firing carefully at the rifle-flashes with his automatic pistol. Jorge had dropped wounded at the first volley and was somewhere out of sight. I knelt beside Benjamin, pulled the pin out of my third bomb and flung it. Ah! No doubt about it that time. The bomb crashed inside the parapet, at the corner, just by the machine-gun nest.

The Fascist fire seemed to have slackened very suddenly. Benjamin leapt to his feet and shouted: 'Forward! Charge!' We dashed up the short steep slope on

which the parapet stood. I say 'dashed'; 'lumbered'
would be a better word; the fact is that you can't move
fast when you are sodden and mudded from head to
foot and weighted down with a heavy rifle and bayonet
and a hundred and fifty cartridges. I took it for granted
that there would be a Fascist waiting for me at the top.
If he fired at that range he could not miss me, and yet
somehow I never expected him to fire, only to try for
me with his bayonet. I seemed to feel in advance the
sensation of our bayonets crossing, and I wondered
whether his arm would be stronger than mine. However, there was no Fascist waiting. With a vague feeling
of relief I found that it was a low parapet and the
sandbags gave a good foothold. As a rule they are
difficult to get over. Everything inside was smashed to
pieces, beams flung all over the place, and great shards
of uralite littered everywhere. Our bombs had wrecked
all the huts and dug-outs. And still there was not a soul
visible. I thought they would be lurking somewhere
underground, and shouted in English (I could not
think of any Spanish at the moment): 'Come on out
of it! Surrender!' No answer. Then a man, a shadowy
figure in the half-light, skipped over the roof of one of
the ruined huts and dashed away to the left. I started
after him, prodding my bayonet ineffectually into the
darkness. As I rounded the corner of the hut I saw a
man – I don't know whether or not it was the same
man as I had seen before – fleeing up the communication-trench that led to the other Fascist position. I
must have been very close to him, for I could see him
clearly. He was bareheaded and seemed to have nothing

on except a blanket which he was clutching round his shoulders. If I had fired I could have blown him to pieces. But for fear of shooting one another we had been ordered to use only bayonets once we were inside the parapet, and in any case I never even thought of firing. Instead, my mind leapt backwards twenty years, to our boxing instructor at school, showing me in vivid pantomime how he had bayoneted a Turk at the Dardanelles. I gripped my rifle by the small of the butt and lunged at the man's back. He was just out of my reach. Another lunge: still out of reach. And for a little distance we proceeded like this, he rushing up the trench and I after him on the ground above, prodding at his shoulder-blades and never quite getting there – a comic memory for me to look back upon, though I suppose it seemed less comic to him.

Of course, he knew the ground better than I and had soon slipped away from me. When I came back the position was full of shouting men. The noise of firing had lessened somewhat. The Fascists were still pouring a heavy fire at us from three sides, but it was coming from a greater distance. We had driven them back for the time being. I remember saying in an oracular manner: 'We can hold this place for half an hour, not more.' I don't know why I picked on half an hour. Looking over the right-hand parapet you could see innumerable greenish rifle-flashes stabbing the darkness; but they were a long way back, a hundred or two hundred yards. Our job now was to search the position and loot anything that was worth looting. Benjamin and some others were already scrabbling among the ruins of a big hut or dug-out in the middle of the position. Benjamin staggered excitedly through the ruined roof, tugging at the rope handle of an ammunition box.

'Comrades! Ammunition! Plenty ammunition here.'

'We don't want ammunition,' said a voice, 'we want rifles.'

This was true. Half our rifles were jammed with mud and unusable. They could be cleaned, but it is dangerous to take the bolt out of a rifle in the darkness; you put it down somewhere and then you lose it. I had a tiny electric torch which my wife had managed to buy in Barcelona, otherwise we had no light of any description between us. A few men with good rifles began a desultory fire at the flashes in the distance. No one dared fire too rapidly; even the best of the rifles were liable to jam if they got too hot. There were about sixteen of us inside the parapet, including one or two who were wounded. A number of wounded, English and Spanish, were lying outside. Patrick O'Hara, a Belfast Irishman who had had some training in first-aid, went to and fro with packets of bandages, binding up the wounded men and, of course, being shot at every time he returned to the parapet, in spite of his indignant shouts of 'POUM!'

We began searching the position. There were several dead men lying about, but I did not stop to examine them. The thing I was after was the machine-gun. All the while when we were lying outside I had been wondering vaguely why the gun did not fire. I flashed my torch inside the machine-gun nest. A bitter disappointment! The gun was not there. Its tripod was there, and various boxes of ammunition and spare parts, but the gun was gone. They must have unscrewed it and carried it off at the first alarm. No doubt they were acting under orders, but it was a stupid and cowardly thing to do, for if they had kept the gun in place they could have slaughtered the whole lot of us. We were furious. We had set our hearts on capturing a machine-gun.

We poked here and there but did not find anything of much value. There were quantities of Fascist bombs lying about – a rather inferior type of bomb, which you touched off by pulling a string – and I put a couple of them in my pocket as souvenirs. It was impossible not to be struck by the bare misery of the Fascist dug-outs. The litter of spare clothes, books, food, petty personal belongings that you saw in our own dug-outs was completely absent; these poor unpaid conscripts seemed to own nothing except blankets and a few soggy hunks of bread. Up at the far end there was a small dug-out which was partly above ground and had a tiny window. We flashed the torch through the window and instantly raised a cheer. A cylindrical object in a leather case, four feet high and six inches in diameter, was leaning against the wall. Obviously the machine-gun barrel. We dashed round and got in at the doorway, to find that the thing in the leather case was not a machine-gun but something which, in our weapon-starved army, was even more precious. It was an enormous telescope, probably of at least sixty or seventy magnifications, with a folding tripod. Such telescopes simply did not exist on our side of the line and they were desperately needed. We brought it out in triumph and leaned it against the parapet, to be carried off later.

At this moment someone shouted that the Fascists were closing in. Certainly the din of firing had grown very much louder. But it was obvious that the Fascists would not counter-attack from the right, which meant crossing no-man's-land and assaulting their own parapet. If they had any sense at all they would come at us from inside the line. I went round to the other side of the dug-outs. The position was roughly horseshoe-shaped, with the dug-outs in the middle, so that we had another parapet covering us on the left. A heavy fire was coming from that direction, but it did not matter greatly. The danger-spot was straight in front, where there was no protection at all. A stream of bullets was passing just overhead. They must be coming from the other Fascist position further up the line; evidently the Shock Troopers had not captured it after all. But this time the noise was deafening. It was the unbroken drum-like roar of massed rifles which I was used to hearing from a little distance; this was the first time I had been in the middle of it. And by now, of course, the firing had spread along the line for miles around. Douglas Thompson, with a wounded arm dangling useless at his side, was leaning against the parapet and firing one-handed at the flashes. Someone whose rifle had jammed was loading for him.

There were four or five of us round this side. It was obvious what we must do. We must drag the sandbags from the front parapet and make a barricade across the unprotected side. And we had got to be quick. The fire was high at present, but they might lower it at any moment; by the flashes all round I could see that we had a hundred or two hundred men against us. We began wrenching the sandbags loose, carrying them twenty yards forward and dumping them into a rough heap. It was a vile job. They were big sandbags, weighing a hundredweight each, and it took every ounce of your strength to prise them loose; and then the rotten sacking split and the damp earth cascaded all over you, down your neck and up your sleeves. I remember feeling a deep horror at everything: the chaos, the darkness, the frightful din, the slithering to and fro in the mud, the struggles with the bursting sandbags – all the time encumbered with my rifle, which I dared not put down for fear of losing it. I even shouted to someone as we staggered along with a bag between us: 'This is war! Isn't it bloody?' Suddenly a succession of tall figures came leaping over the front parapet. As they came nearer we saw that they wore the uniform of the Shock Troopers, and we cheered, thinking they were reinforcements. However, there were only four of them, three Germans and a Spaniard. We heard afterwards what had happened to the Shock Troopers. They did not know the ground and in the darkness had been led to the wrong place, where they were caught on the Fascist wire and numbers of them were shot down. These were four who had got lost, luckily for themselves. The Germans did not speak a word of English, French, or Spanish. With difficulty and much gesticulation we explained what we were doing and got them to help us in building the barricade.

The Fascists had brought up a machine-gun now. You could see it spitting like a squib a hundred or two hundred yards away; the bullets came over us with a steady, frosty crackle. Before long we had flung enough sandbags into place to make a low breastwork behind which the few men who were on this side of the position could lie down and fire. I was kneeling behind them. A mortar-shell whizzed over and crashed somewhere in no-man's-land. That was another danger, but it would take them some minutes to find our range. Now that we had finished wrestling with those beastly sandbags it was not bad fun in a way; the noise, the darkness, the flashes approaching, our own men blazing back at the flashes. One even had time to think a little. I remember wondering whether I was frightened, and deciding that I was not. Outside, where I was probably in less danger, I had been half sick with fright. Suddenly there was another shout that the Fascists were closing in. There was no doubt about it this time, the rifle-flashes were much nearer. I saw a flash hardly twenty yards away. Obviously they were working their way up the communication-trench. At twenty yards they were within easy bombing range; there were eight or nine of us bunched together and a single well-placed bomb would blow us all to fragments. Bob Smillie, the blood running down his face from a small wound, sprang to his knee and flung a bomb. We cowered, waiting for the crash. The fuse fizzled red as it sailed through the air, but the bomb failed to explode. (At least a quarter of these bombs were duds.) I had no bombs left except the Fascist ones and I was not certain how these worked. I shouted to the others to know if anyone had a bomb to spare. Douglas Moyle felt in his pocket and passed one across. I flung it and threw myself on my face. By one of those strokes of luck that happen about once in a year I had managed to drop the bomb almost exactly where the rifle had flashed. There was the roar of the explosion and then, instantly, a diabolical outcry of screams and groans. We had got one of them, anyway; I don't know whether he was killed, but certainly he was badly hurt. Poor wretch, poor wretch! I felt a vague sorrow as I heard him screaming. But at the same instant, in the dim light of the rifle-flashes, I saw or thought I saw a figure standing near the place where the rifle had flashed. I threw up my rifle and let fly. Another scream, but I think it was still the effect of the bomb. Several more bombs were thrown. The next rifle-flashes we saw were a long way off, a hundred yards or more. So we had driven them back, temporarily at least.

Everyone began cursing and saying why the hell didn't they send us some supports. With a sub-machine-gun or twenty men with clean rifles we could hold this place against a battalion. At this moment Paddy Donovan, who was second-in-command to Benjamin and had been sent back for orders, climbed over the front parapet.

'Hi! Come on out of it! All men to retire at once!'

'What?'

'Retire! Get out of it!'

'Why?'

'Orders. Back to our own lines double-quick.'

People were already climbing over the front parapet. Several of them were struggling with a heavy ammunition box. My mind flew to the telescope which I had left leaning against the parapet on the other side of the position. But at this moment I saw that the four Shock Troopers, acting I suppose on some mysterious orders they had received beforehand, had begun running up the communication-trench. It led to the other Fascist position and – if they got there – to certain death. They were disappearing into the darkness. I ran after them, trying to think of the Spanish for 'retire'; finally I shouted, *'Atrás! Atrás!'*, which perhaps conveyed the right meaning. The Spaniard understood it and brought the others back. Paddy was waiting at the parapet.

'Come on, hurry up.'

'But the telescope!'

'Bugger the telescope! Benjamin's waiting outside.'

We climbed out. Paddy held the wire aside for me. As soon as we got away from the shelter of the Fascist parapet we were under a devilish fire that seemed to be coming at us from every direction. Part of it, I do not doubt, came from our own side, for everyone was firing all along the line. Whichever way we turned a fresh stream of bullets swept past; we were driven this way and that in the darkness like a flock of sheep. It did not make it any easier that we were dragging a captured box of ammunition – one of those boxes that hold 1750 rounds and weigh about a hundredweight – besides a box of bombs and several Fascist rifles. In a few minutes, although the distance from parapet to parapet was not two hundred yards and most of us knew the ground, we were completely lost. We found ourselves slithering about in a muddy field, knowing nothing except that bullets were coming from both sides. There was no moon to go by, but the sky was growing a little lighter. Our lines lay east of Huesca; I wanted to stay where we were till the first crack of dawn showed us which was east and which was west; but the others were against it. We slithered onwards, changing our direction several times and taking it in turns to haul at the ammunition-box. At last we saw the low flat line of a parapet looming in front of us. It might be ours or it might be the Fascists'; nobody had the dimmest idea which way we were going. Benjamin crawled on his belly through some tall whitish weeds till he was about twenty yards from the parapet and tried a challenge. A shout of 'POUM!' answered him. We jumped to our feet, found our way along the parapet, slopped once more through the irrigation ditch – splash-gurgle! – and were in safety.

Kopp was waiting inside the parapet with a few Spaniards. The doctor and the stretchers were gone. It appeared that all the wounded had been got in except Jorge and one of our own men, Hiddlestone by name, who were missing. Kopp was pacing up and down, very pale. Even the fat folds at the back of his neck were pale; he was paying no attention to the bullets that streamed over the low parapet and cracked close to his head. Most of us were squatting behind the parapet for cover. Kopp was muttering. *'Jorge! Coño! Jorge!'*

And then in English. 'If Jorge is gone it is terreeble, terreeble!' Jorge was his personal friend and one of his best officers. Suddenly he turned to us and asked for five volunteers, two English and three Spanish, to go and look for the missing men. Moyle and I volunteered with three Spaniards.

As we got outside the Spaniards murmured that it was getting dangerously light. This was true enough; the sky was dimly blue. There was a tremendous noise of excited voices coming from the Fascist redoubt. Evidently they had reoccupied the place in much greater force than before. We were sixty or seventy yards from the parapet when they must have seen or heard us, for they sent over a heavy burst of fire which made us drop on our faces. One of them flung a bomb over the parapet – a sure sign of panic. We were lying in the grass, waiting for an opportunity to move on, when we either heard or thought we heard – I have no doubt it was pure imagination, but it seemed real enough at the time – that the Fascist voices were much closer. They had left the parapet and were coming after us. 'Run!' I yelled to Moyle, and jumped to my feet. And heavens, how I ran! I had thought earlier in the night that you can't run when you are sodden from head to foot and weighted down with a rifle and cartridges; I learned now you can *always* run when you think you have fifty or a hundred armed men after you. But if I could run fast, others could run faster. In my flight something that might have been a shower of meteors sped past me. It was the three Spaniards, who had been in front. They were back to our own parapet before they stopped and I could catch up with them. The truth was that our nerves were all to pieces. I knew, however, that in a half-light one man is invisible where five are clearly visible, so I went back alone. I managed to get to the outer wire and searched the ground as well as I could, which was not very well, for I had to lie on my belly. There was no sign of Jorge or Hiddlestone, so I crept back. We learned afterwards that both Jorge and Hiddlestone had been taken to the dressing-station earlier. Jorge was lightly wounded through the shoulder. Hiddlestone had received a dreadful wound – a bullet which travelled right up his left arm, breaking the bone in several places; as he lay helpless on the ground a bomb had burst near him and torn various other parts of his body. He recovered, I am glad to say. Later he told me that he had worked his way some distance lying on his back, then had clutched hold of a wounded Spaniard and they had helped one another in.

It was getting light now. Along the line for miles around a ragged meaningless fire was thundering, like the rain that goes on raining after a storm. I remember the desolate look of everything, the morasses of mud, the weeping poplar trees, the yellow water in the trench-bottoms; and men's exhausted faces, unshaven, streaked with mud and blackened to the eyes with smoke. When I got back to my dug-out the three men I shared it with were already fast asleep. They had flung themselves down with all their equipment on and their muddy rifles clutched against them. Everything was sodden, inside the dug-out as well as outside. By long searching I managed to collect enough chips of dry wood to make a tiny fire. Then I smoked the cigar which I had been hoarding and which, surprisingly enough, had not got broken during the night.

Afterwards we learned that the action had been a success, as such things go. It was merely a raid to make the Fascists divert troops from the other side of Huesca, where the Anarchists were attacking again. I had judged that the Fascists had thrown a hundred or two hundred men into the counter-attack, but a deserter told us later on that it was six hundred. I dare say he was lying – deserters, for obvious reasons, often try to curry favour. It was a great pity about the telescope. The thought of losing that beautiful bit of loot worries me even now.

VII

Getting back to Barcelona, after three and a half months at the front, there was an abrupt and startling change of atmosphere. In the train, all the way to Barcelona, the atmosphere of the front persisted; the dirt, the noise, the discomfort, the ragged clothes, the feeling of privation, comradeship and equality. The train, already full of militiamen when it left Barbastro, was invaded by more and more peasants at every station on the line; peasants with bundles of vegetables, with terrified fowls which they carried head-downwards, with sacks which looped and writhed all over the floor and were discovered to be full of live rabbits – finally with a quite considerable flock of sheep which were driven into the compartments and wedged into every empty space. The militiamen shouted revolutionary songs which drowned the rattle of the train and kissed their hands or waved red and black handkerchiefs to every pretty girl along the line. Bottles of wine and of anis, the filthy Aragonese liqueur, travelled from hand to hand. With the Spanish goatskin water bottles you can squirt a jet of wine right across a railway carriage into your friend's mouth, which saves a lot of trouble. Next to me a black-eyed boy of fifteen was recounting sensational and, I do not doubt, completely untrue stories of his own exploits at the front to two old leather-faced peasants who listened open-mouthed. Presently the peasants undid their bundles and gave us some sticky dark-red wine. Everyone was profoundly happy, more happy than I can convey. But when the train had rolled through Sabadell and into Barcelona, we stepped into an atmosphere that was scarcely less alien and hostile to us and our kind than if this had been Paris or London.

Everyone who has made two visits, at intervals of months, to Barcelona during the war has remarked upon the extraordinary changes that took place in it. And curiously enough, whether they went there first in August and again in January, or, like myself, first in December and again in April, the thing they said was always the same: that the revolutionary atmosphere had vanished. No doubt to anyone who had been there in August, when the blood was scarcely dry in the streets and militia were quartered in the smart hotels, Barcelona in December would have seemed bourgeois; to me, fresh from England, it was liker to a workers' city than anything I had conceived possible. Now the tide had rolled back. Once again it was an ordinary city, a little pinched and chipped by war, but with no outward sign of working-class predominance.

The change in the aspect of the crowds was startling. The militia uniform and the blue overalls had almost disappeared; everyone seemed to be wearing the smart summer suits in which Spanish tailors specialize. Fat prosperous men, elegant women, and sleek cars were everywhere. (It appeared that there were still no private cars; nevertheless, anyone who 'was anyone' seemed able to command a car.) The officers of the new Popular Army, a type that had scarcely existed when I left Barcelona, swarmed in surprising numbers. The Popular Army was officered at the rate of one officer to ten men. A certain number of these officers had served in the militia and been brought back from the front for technical instruction, but the majority were young men who had gone to the School of War in preference to joining the militia. Their relation to their men was not quite the same as in a bourgeois army, but there was a definite social difference, expressed by the difference of pay and uniform. The men wore a kind of coarse brown overalls, the officers wore an elegant khaki uniform with a tight waist, like a British Army officer's uniform, only a little more so. I do not suppose that more than one in twenty of them had yet been to the front, but all of them had automatic pistols strapped to their belts; we, at the front, could not get pistols for love or money. As we made our way up the street I noticed that people were staring at our dirty exteriors. Of course, like all men who have been several months in the line, we were a dreadful sight. I was conscious of looking like a scarecrow. My leather jacket was in tatters, my woollen cap had lost its shape and slid perpetually over one eye, my boots consisted of very little beyond splayed-out uppers. All of us were in more or less the same state, and in addition we were dirty and unshaven, so it was no wonder that the people stared. But it dismayed me a little, and brought it home to me that some queer things had been happening in the last three months.

During the next few days I discovered by innumerable signs that my first impression had not been wrong. A deep change had come over the town. There were two facts that were the keynote of all else. One was that the people – the civil population – had lost much of their interest in the war; the other was that the normal division of society into rich and poor, upper class and lower class, was reasserting itself.

The general indifference to the war was surprising and rather disgusting. It horrified people who came to Barcelona from Madrid or even from Valencia. Partly it was due to the remoteness of Barcelona from the actual fighting; I noticed the same thing a month later in Tarragona, where the ordinary life of a smart seaside town was continuing almost undisturbed. But it was significant that all over Spain voluntary enlistment had dwindled from about January onwards. In Catalonia, in February, there had been a wave of enthusiasm over the first big drive for the Popular Army, but it had not led to any great increase in recruiting. The war was only six months old or thereabouts when the Spanish Government had to resort to conscription, which would be natural in a foreign war, but seems anomalous in a civil war. Undoubtedly it was bound up with the disappointment of the revolutionary hopes with which the war had started. The trade union members who formed themselves into militias and chased the Fascists back to Saragossa in the first few weeks of war had done so largely because they believed themselves to be fighting for working-class control; but it was becoming more and more obvious that working-class control was a lost cause, and the common people, especially the town proletariat, who have to fill the ranks in any war, civil or foreign, could not be blamed for a certain apathy. Nobody wanted to lose the war, but the majority were chiefly anxious for it to be over.

VIII

About midday on 3 May a friend crossing the lounge of the hotel said casually: 'There's been some kind of trouble at the Telephone Exchange, I hear.' For some reason I paid no attention to it at the time.

That afternoon, between three and four, I was half-way down the Ramblas when I heard several rifle-shots behind me. I turned round and saw some youths, with rifles in their hands and the red and black handkerchiefs of the Anarchists round their throats, edging up a side-street that ran off the Ramblas northward. They were evidently exchanging shots with someone in a tall octagonal tower – a church, I think – that commanded the side street. I thought instantly: 'It's started!' But I thought it without any very great feeling of surprise – for days past everyone had been expecting 'it' to start at any moment. I realized that I must get back to the hotel at once and see if my wife was all right. But the knot of Anarchists round the opening of the side street were motioning the people back and shouting to them not to cross the line of fire. More shots rang out. The bullets from the tower were flying across the street and a crowd of panic-stricken people was rushing down the Ramblas, away from the firing; up and down the street you could hear snap-snap-snap as the shop-keepers slammed the steel shutters over their windows. I saw two Popular Army officers retreating cautiously from tree to tree with their hands on their revolvers. In front of me the crowd was surging into the Metro station in the middle of the Ramblas to take cover. I immediately decided not to follow them. It might mean being trapped underground for hours.

At this moment an American doctor who had been with us at the front ran up to me and grabbed me by the arm. He was greatly excited.

'Come on, we must get down to the Hotel Falcón.' (The Hotel Falcón was a sort of boarding house maintained by the POUM and used chiefly by militiamen on leave.) 'The POUM chaps will be meeting there. The trouble's starting. We must hang together.'

'But what the devil is it all about?' I said.

The doctor was hauling me along by the arm. He was too excited to give a very clear statement. It appeared that he had been in the Plaza de Cataluña when several lorryloads of armed Assault Guards had driven up to the Telephone Exchange, which was operated mainly by CNT[4] workers, and made a sudden assault upon it. Then some Anarchists had arrived and there had been a general affray. I gathered that the 'trouble' earlier in the day had been a demand by the Government to hand over the Telephone Exchange, which, of course, was refused.

As we moved down the street a lorry raced past us from the opposite direction. It was full of Anarchists with rifles in their hands. In front a ragged youth was lying on a pile of mattresses behind a light machine-gun. When we got to the Hotel Falcón, which was at the bottom of the Ramblas, a crowd of people was seething in the entrance hall; there was great confusion, nobody seemed to know what we were expected to do, and nobody was armed except the handful of Shock Troopers who usually acted as guards for the building. I went across to the Comité Local of the POUM, which was almost opposite. Upstairs, in the room where militiamen normally went to draw their pay, another crowd was seething. A tall, pale, rather handsome man of about thirty, in civilian clothes, was trying to restore order and handing out belts and cartridge-

[4] CNT (Confederación Nacional de Trabajo; Anarcho – Syndicalist Trades Union).

boxes from a box in the corner. There seemed to be no rifles as yet. The doctor had disappeared – I believe there had already been casualties and a call for doctors – but another Englishman had arrived. Presently, from an inner office, the tall man and some others began bringing out armfuls of rifles and handing them round. The other Englishman and myself, as foreigners, were slightly under suspicion and at first nobody would give us a rifle. Then a militiaman whom I had known at the front arrived and recognized me, after which we were given rifles and a few clips of cartridges, somewhat grudgingly.

There was a sound of firing in the distance and the streets were completely empty of people. Everyone said that it was impossible to go up the Ramblas. The Assault Guards had seized buildings in commanding positions and were letting fly at everyone who passed. I would have risked it and gone back to the hotel, but there was a vague idea floating round that the Comité Local was likely to be attacked at any moment and we had better stand by. All over the building, on the stairs and on the pavement outside, small knots of people were standing and talking excitedly. No one seemed to have a very clear idea of what was happening. All I could gather was that the Assault Guards had attacked the Telephone Exchange and seized various strategic spots that commanded other buildings belonging to the workers. There was a general impression that the Assault Guards were 'after' the CNT and the working class generally. It was noticeable that, at this stage, no one seemed to put the blame on the Government. The poorer classes in Barcelona looked upon the Assault Guards as something rather resembling the Black and Tans, and it seemed to be taken for granted that they had started this attack on their own initiative. Once I had heard how things stood I felt easier in my mind. The issue was clear enough. On one side the CNT, on the other side the police. I have no particular love for the idealized 'worker' as he appears in the bourgeois Communist's mind, but when I see an actual flesh-and-blood worker in conflict with his natural enemy, the policeman, I do not have to ask myself which side I am on.

A long time passed and nothing seemed to be happening at our end of the town. It did not occur to me that I could ring up the hotel and find out whether my wife was all right; I took it for granted that the Telephone Exchange would have stopped working – though, as a matter of fact, it was only out of action for a couple of hours. There seemed to be about three hundred people in the two buildings. Predominantly they were people of the poorest class, from the back-streets down by the quays; there was a number of women among them, some of them carrying babies, and a crowd of little ragged boys. I fancy that many of them had no notion what was happening and had simply fled into the POUM buildings for protection. There was also a number of militiamen on leave, and a sprinkling of foreigners. As far as I could estimate, there were only about sixty rifles between the lot of us. The office upstairs was ceaselessly besieged by a crowd of people who were demanding rifles and being told that there were none left. The younger militia boys, who seemed to regard the whole affair as a kind of picnic, were prowling round and trying to wheedle or steal rifles from anyone who had them. It was not long before one of them got my rifle away from me by a clever dodge and immediately made himself scarce. So I was unarmed again, except for my tiny automatic pistol, for which I had only one clip of cartridges.

It grew dark, I was getting hungry, and seemingly there was no food in the Falcón. My friend and I slipped out to his hotel, which was not far away, to get some dinner. The streets were utterly dark and silent, not a soul stirring, steel shutters drawn over all the shop windows, but no barricades built yet. There was a great fuss before they would let us into the hotel, which was locked and barred. When we got back I learned that the Telephone Exchange was working and went to the telephone in the office upstairs to ring up my wife. Characteristically, there was no telephone directory in the building, and I did not know the number of the Hotel Continental; after searching from room to room for about an hour I came upon a guide-book which gave me the number. I could not make contact with my wife, but I managed to get hold of John McNair, the ILP representative in Barcelona. He told me that all was well, nobody had been shot, and asked me if we were all right at the Comité Local. I said that we should be all right if we had some cigarettes. I only meant this as a joke; nevertheless half an hour later McNair appeared with two packets of Lucky Strike. He had braved the pitch-dark streets, roamed by Anarchist patrols who had twice stopped him at the pistol's point and examined his papers. I shall not forget this small act of heroism. We were very glad of the cigarettes.

They had placed armed guards at most of the windows, and in the street below a little group of Shock Troopers were stopping and questioning the few passers-by. An Anarchist patrol car drove up, bristling with weapons. Beside the driver a beautiful dark-haired girl of about eighteen was nursing a sub-machine gun across her knees. I spent a long time wandering about the building, a great rambling place of which it was impossible to learn the geography. Everywhere was the usual litter, the broken furniture and torn paper that seem to be the inevitable products of revolution. All over the place people were sleeping; on a broken sofa in a passage two poor women from the quayside were peacefully snoring. The place had been a cabaret-theatre before the POUM took it over. There were raised stages in several of the rooms; on one of them was a desolate grand piano. Finally I discovered what I was looking for – the armoury. I did not know how this affair was going to turn out, and I badly wanted a weapon. I had heard it said so often that all the rival parties, PSUC, POUM, and CNT–FAI alike, were hoarding arms in Barcelona, that I could not believe that two of the principal POUM buildings contained only the fifty or sixty rifles that I had seen. The room which acted as an armoury was unguarded and had a flimsy door: another Englishman and myself had no difficulty in prising it open. When we got inside we found that what they had told us was true – there *were* no more weapons. All we found there were about two dozen small-bore rifles of an obsolete pattern and a few shotguns, with no cartridges for any of them. I went up to the office and asked if they had any spare pistol ammunition: they had none. There were a few boxes of bombs, however, which one of the Anarchist patrol cars had brought us. I put a couple in one of my cartridge-boxes. They were a crude type of bomb, ignited by rubbing a sort of match at the top and very liable to go off of their own accord.

People were sprawling asleep all over the floor. In one room a baby was crying, crying ceaselessly. Though this was May the night was getting cold. On one of the cabaret-stages the curtains were still up, so I ripped a curtain down with my knife, rolled myself up in it and had a few hours' sleep. My sleep was disturbed, I remember, by the thought of those beastly bombs, which might blow me into the air if I rolled on them too vigorously. At three in the morning the tall handsome man who seemed to be in command woke me up, gave me a rifle and put me on guard at one of the windows. He told me that Salas, the Chief of Police responsible for the attack on the Telephone Exchange, had been placed under arrest. (Actually, as we learned later, he had only been deprived of his post. Nevertheless the news confirmed the general impression that the Assault Guards had acted without orders.) As soon as it was dawn the people downstairs began building two barricades, one outside the Comité Local and the other outside the Hotel Falcón. The Barcelona streets are paved with square cobbles, easily built up into a wall, and under the cobbles is a kind of shingle that is good for filling sandbags. The building of those barricades was a strange and wonderful sight; I would have given something to be able to photograph it. With the kind of passionate energy that Spaniards display when they have definitely decided to begin upon any job of work, long lines of men, women, and quite small children were tearing up the cobblestones, hauling them along in a hand-cart that had been found some-where, and staggering to and fro under heavy sacks of sand. In the doorway of the Comité Local a German-Jewish girl, in a pair of militiaman's trousers whose knee-buttons just reached her ankles, was watching with a smile. In a couple of hours the barricades were head-high, with riflemen posted at the loopholes, and behind one barricade a fire was burning and men were frying eggs.

They had taken my rifle away again, and there seemed to be nothing that one could usefully do. Another Englishman and myself decided to go back to the Hotel Continental. There was a lot of firing in the distance, but seemingly none in the Ramblas. On the way up we looked in at the food-market. A very few stalls had opened; they were besieged by a crowd of people from the working-class quarters south of the Ramblas. Just as we got there, there was a heavy crash of rifle-fire outside, some panes of glass in the roof were shivered, and the crowd went flying for the back exits. A few stalls remained open, however; we man-aged to get a cup of coffee each and buy a wedge of goat's-milk cheese which I tucked in beside my bombs. A few days later I was very glad of that cheese.

At the street-corner where I had seen the Anarchists begin firing the day before a barricade was now standing. The man behind it (I was on the other side of the street) shouted to me to be careful. The Assault Guards in the church tower were firing indiscriminately at everyone who passed. I paused and then crossed the opening at a run; sure enough, a bullet cracked past me, uncomfortably close. When I neared the POUM Executive Building, still on the other side of the road, there were fresh shouts of warning from some Shock Troopers standing in the doorway – shouts which, at the moment, I did not understand. There were trees and a newspaper kiosk between myself and the building (streets of this type in Spain have a broad walk running down the middle), and I could not see what they were pointing at. I went up to the Continental, made sure that all was well, washed my face and then went back to the POUM Executive Building (it was about a hundred yards down the street) to ask for orders. By this time the roar of rifle and machine-gun fire from various directions was almost comparable to the din of a battle. I had just found Kopp and was asking him what we were supposed to do when there was a series of appalling crashes down below. The din was so loud that I made sure someone must be firing at us with a field-gun. Actually it was only hand grenades, which make double their usual noise when they burst among stone buildings.

Kopp glanced out of the window, cocked his stick

behind his back, said: 'Let us investigate,' and strolled down the stairs in his usual unconcerned manner, I following. Just inside the doorway a group of Shock Troopers were bowling bombs down the pavement as though playing skittles. The bombs were bursting twenty yards away with a frightful, ear-splitting crash which was mixed up with the banging of rifles. Half across the street, from behind the newspaper kiosk, a head – it was the head of an American militiaman whom I knew well – was sticking up, for all the world like a coconut at a fair. It was only afterwards that I grasped what was really happening. Next door to the POUM building there was a café with an hotel above it, called the Café Moka. The day before twenty or thirty armed Assault Guards had entered the café and then, when the fighting started, had suddenly seized the building and barricaded themselves in. Presumably they had been ordered to seize the café as a preliminary to attacking the POUM offices later. Early in the morning they had attempted to come out, shots had been exchanged and one Shock Trooper was badly wounded and an Assault Guard killed. The Assault Guards had fled back into the café, but when the American came down the street they had opened fire on him, though he was not armed. The American had flung himself behind the kiosk for cover, and the Shock Troopers were flinging bombs at the Assault Guards to drive them indoors again.

Kopp took in the scene at a glance, pushed his way forward and hauled back a red-haired German Shock Trooper who was just drawing the pin out of a bomb with his teeth. He shouted to everyone to stand back from the doorway, and told us in several languages that we had got to avoid bloodshed. Then he stepped out onto the pavement and, in sight of the Assault Guards, ostentatiously took off his pistol and laid it on the ground. Two Spanish militia officers did the same, and the three of them walked slowly up to the doorway where the Assault Guards were huddling. It was a thing I would not have done for twenty pounds. They were walking, unarmed, up to men who were frightened out of their wits and had loaded guns in their hands. An Assault Guard, in shirt-sleeves and livid with fright, came out of the door to parley with Kopp. He kept pointing in an agitated manner at two unexploded bombs that were lying on the pavement. Kopp came back and told us we had better touch the bombs off. Lying there, they were a danger to anyone who passed. A Shock Trooper fired his rifle at one of the bombs and burst it, then fired at the other and missed. I asked him to give me his rifle, knelt down and let fly at the second bomb. I also missed it, I am sorry to say. This was the only shot I fired during the disturbances. The pavement was covered with broken glass from the sign over the Café Moka, and two cars that were parked outside, one of them Kopp's official car, had been riddled with bullets and their windscreens smashed by bursting bombs.

Kopp took me upstairs again and explained the situation. We had got to defend the POUM buildings if they were attacked, but the POUM leaders had sent instructions that we were to stand on the defensive and not open fire if we could possibly avoid it. Immediately opposite there was a cinematograph, called the Poliorama, with a museum above it, and at the top, high above the general level of the roofs, a small observatory with twin domes. The domes commanded the street, and a few men posted up there with rifles could prevent any attack on the POUM buildings. The caretakers at the cinema were CNT members and would let us come and go. As for the Assault Guards in the Café Moka, there would be no trouble with them; they did not want to fight and would be only too glad to live and let live. Kopp repeated that our orders were not to fire unless we were fired on ourselves or our buildings attacked. I gathered, though he did not say so, that the POUM leaders were furious at being dragged into this affair, but felt that they had got to stand by the CNT

They had already placed guards in the observatory. The next three days and nights I spent continuously on the roof of the Poliorama, except for brief intervals when I slipped across to the hotel for meals. I was in no danger, I suffered from nothing worse than hunger and boredom, yet it was one of the most unbearable periods of my whole life. I think few experiences could be more sickening, more disillusioning or, finally, more nerve-racking than those evil days of street warfare.

I used to sit on the roof marvelling at the folly of it all. From the little windows in the observatory you could see for miles around – vista after vista of tall slender buildings, glass domes and fantastic curly roofs with brilliant green and copper tiles; over to eastward the glittering pale blue sea – the first glimpse of the sea that I had had since coming to Spain. And the whole huge town of a million people was locked in a sort of violent inertia, a nightmare of noise without movement. The sunlit streets were quite empty. Nothing was happening except the streaming of bullets from barricades and sandbagged windows. Not a vehicle was stirring in the streets; here and there along the Ramblas the trams stood motionless where their drivers had jumped out of them when the fighting started. And all the while the devilish noise, echoing from thousands of stone buildings, went on and on and on, like a tropical rainstorm. Crack-crack, rattle-rattle, roar – sometimes it died away to a few shots, sometimes it quickened to a deafening fusillade, but it never stopped while daylight lasted, and punctually next dawn it started again.

What the devil was happening, who was fighting whom and who was winning, was at first very difficult to discover. The people of Barcelona are so used to street-fighting and so familiar with the local geography that they know by a kind of instinct which political party will hold which streets and which buildings. A foreigner is at a hopeless disadvantage. Looking out from the observatory, I could grasp that the Ramblas, which is one of the principal streets of the town, formed a dividing line. To the right of the Ramblas the working-class quarters were solidly Anarchist; to the left a confused fight was going on among the tortuous by-streets, but on that side the PSUC and the Assault Guards were more or less in control. Up at our end of the Ramblas, round the Plaza de Cataluña, the position was so complicated that it would have been quite unintelligible if every building had not flown a party flag. The principal landmark here was the Hotel Colón, the headquarters of the PSUC, dominating the Plaza de Cataluña. In a window near the last O but one in the huge 'Hotel Colón' that sprawled across its face they had a machine-gun that could sweep the square with deadly effect. A hundred yards to the right of us, down the Ramblas, the JSU, the youth league of the PSUC (corresponding to the Young Communist League in England) were holding a big department store whose sandbagged side-windows fronted our observatory. They had hauled down their red flag and hoisted the Catalan national flag. On the Telephone Exchange, the starting-point of all the trouble, the Catalan national flag and the Anarchist flag were flying side by side. Some kind of temporary compromise had been arrived at there, the exchange was working uninterruptedly and there was no firing from the building.

In our position it was strangely peaceful. The Assault Guards in the Café Moka had drawn down the steel curtains and piled up the café furniture to make a barricade. Later half a dozen of them came onto the roof, opposite to ourselves, and built another barricade of mattresses, over which they hung a Catalan national flag. But it was obvious that they had no wish to start a fight. Kopp had made a definite agreement with them: if they did not fire at us we would not fire at them. He had grown quite friendly with the Assault

Guards by this time, and had been to visit them several times in the Café Moka. Naturally they had looted everything drinkable the café possessed, and they made Kopp a present of fifteen bottles of beer. In return Kopp had actually given them one of our rifles to make up for one they had somehow lost on the previous day. Nevertheless, it was a queer feeling sitting on that roof. Sometimes I was merely bored with the whole affair, paid no attention to the hellish noise, and spent hours reading a succession of Penguin Library books which, luckily, I had bought a few days earlier; sometimes I was very conscious of the armed men watching me fifty yards away. It was a little like being in the trenches again: several times I caught myself, from force of habit, speaking of the Assault Guards as 'the Fascists'. There were generally about six of us up there. We placed a man on guard in each of the observatory towers, and the rest of us sat on the lead roof below where there was no cover except a stone palisade. I was well aware that at any moment the Assault Guards might receive telephone orders to open fire. They had agreed to give us warning before doing so, but there was no certainty that they would keep to their agreement. Only once, however, did trouble look like starting. One of the Assault Guards opposite knelt down and began firing across the barricade. I was on guard in the observatory at the time. I trained my rifle on him and shouted across:

'Hi! Don't you shoot at us!'

'What?'

'Don't you fire at us or we'll fire back!'

'No, no! I wasn't firing at you. Look – down there!'

He motioned with his rifle towards the side street that ran past the bottom of our building. Sure enough, a youth in blue overalls, with a rifle in his hand, was dodging round the corner. Evidently he had just taken a shot at the Assault Guards on the roof.

'I was firing at him. He fired first.' (I believe this was true.) We don't want to shoot you. We're only workers, the same as you are.'

He made the anti-Fascist salute, which I returned. I shouted across:

'Have you got any more beer left?'

'No, it's all gone.'

The same day, for no apparent reason, a man in the JSU building further down the street suddenly raised his rifle and let fly at me when I was leaning out of the window. Perhaps I made a tempting mark. I did not fire back. Though he was only a hundred yards away the bullet went so wide that it did not even hit the roof of the observatory. As usual, Spanish standards of marksmanship had saved me. I was fired at several times from this building.

The devilish racket of firing went on and on. But so far as I could see, and from all I heard, the fighting was defensive on both sides. People simply remained in their buildings or behind their barricades and blazed away at the people opposite. About half a mile away from us there was a street where some of the main offices of the CNT and the UGT were almost exactly facing one another; from that direction the volume of noise was terrific. I passed down that street the day after the fighting was over and the panes of the shop-windows were like sieves. (Most of the shopkeepers in Barcelona had their windows criss-crossed with strips of paper, so that when a bullet hit a pane it did not shiver to pieces.) Sometimes the rattle of rifle and machine-gun fire was punctuated by the crash of hand-grenades. And at long intervals, perhaps a dozen times in all, there were tremendously heavy explosions which at the time I could not account for; they sounded like aerial bombs, but that was impossible, for there were no aeroplanes about. I was told afterwards – quite possibly it was true – that *agents provocateurs* were touching off masses of explosive in order to increase the general noise and panic. There was, however, no artillery-fire. I was listening for this, for if the guns began to fire it would mean that the affair was becoming serious (artillery is the determining factor in street warfare). Afterwards there were wild tales in the newspapers about batteries of guns firing in the streets, but no one was able to point to a building that had been hit by a shell. In any case the sound of gunfire is unmistakable if one is used to it.

Almost from the start food was running short. With difficulty and under cover of darkness (for the Assault Guards were constantly sniping into the Ramblas) food was brought from the Hotel Falcón for the fifteen or twenty militiamen who were in the POUM Executive Building, but there was barely enough to go round, and as many of us as possible went to the Hotel Continental for our meals. The Continental had been 'collectivized' by the Generalidad and not, like most of the hotels, by the CNT or UGT, and it was regarded as neutral ground. No sooner had the fighting started than the hotel filled to the brim with a most extraordinary collection of people. There were foreign journalists, political suspects of every shade, an American airman in the service of the Government, various Communist agents, including a fat, sinister-looking Russian, said to be an agent of the Ogpu, who was nicknamed Charlie Chan and wore attached to his waistband a revolver and a neat little bomb, some families of well-to-do Spaniards who looked like Fascist sympathizers, two or three wounded men from the International Column, a gang of lorry drivers from some huge French lorries which had been carrying a load of oranges back to France and had been held up by the fighting, and a number of Popular Army officers. The Popular Army, as a body, remained neutral throughout the fighting, though a few soldiers slipped away from the barracks and took part as individuals; on the Tuesday morning I had seen a couple of them at the POUM barricades. At the beginning, before the food-shortage became acute and the newspapers began stirring up hatred, there was a tendency to regard the whole affair as a joke. This was the kind of thing that happened every year in Barcelona, people were saying. George Tioli, an Italian journalist, a great friend of ours, came in with his trousers drenched with blood. He had gone out to see what was happening and had been binding up a wounded man on the pavement when someone playfully tossed a hand grenade at him, fortunately not wounding him seriously. I remember his remarking that the Barcelona paving stones ought to be numbered; it would save such a lot of trouble in building and demolishing barricades. And I remember a couple of men from the International Column sitting in my room at the hotel when I came in tired, hungry, and dirty after a night on guard. Their attitude was completely neutral. If they had been good party-men they would, I suppose, have urged me to change sides, or even have pinioned me and taken away the bombs of which my pockets were full; instead they merely commiserated with me for having to spend my leave in doing guard-duty on a roof. The general attitude was: 'This is only a dust-up between the Anarchists and the police – it doesn't mean anything.' In spite of the extent of the fighting and the number of casualties I believe this was nearer the truth than the official version which represented the affair as a planned rising.

It was about Wednesday (5 May) that a change seemed to come over things. The shuttered streets looked ghastly. A very few pedestrians, forced abroad for one reason or another, crept to and fro, flourishing white handkerchiefs, and at a spot in the middle of the Ramblas that was safe from bullets some men were crying newspapers to the empty street. On Tuesday *Solidaridad Obrera*, the Anarchist paper, had described the attack on the Telephone Exchange as a 'monstrous provocation' (or words to that effect), but on Wednesday it changed its tune and began imploring everyone to go back to work. The Anarchist leaders were broadcasting the same message. The office of *La Batalla*, the

POUM paper, which was not defended, had been raided and seized by the Assault Guards at about the same time as the Telephone Exchange, but the paper was being printed, and a few copies distributed, from another address. It urged everyone to remain at the barricades. People were divided in their minds and wondering uneasily how the devil this was going to end. I doubt whether anyone left the barricades as yet, but everyone was sick of the meaningless fighting, which could obviously lead to no real decision, because no one wanted this to develop into a full-sized civil war which might mean losing the war against Franco. I heard this fear expressed on all sides. So far as one could gather from what people were saying at the time the CNT rank and file wanted, and had wanted from the beginning, only two things: the handing back of the Telephone Exchange and the disarming of the Assault Guards. If the Generalidad had promised to do these two things, and also promised to put an end to the food profiteering, there is little doubt that the barricades would have been down in two hours. But it was obvious that the Generalidad was not going to give in. Ugly rumours were flying round. It was said that the Valencia Government was sending six thousand men to occupy Barcelona, and that five thousand Anarchist and POUM troops had left the Aragón front to oppose them. Only the first of these rumours was true. Watching from the observatory tower we saw the low grey shapes of warships closing in upon the harbour. Douglas Moyle, who had been a sailor, said that they looked like British destroyers. As a matter of fact they *were* British destroyers, though we did not learn this till afterwards.

That evening we heard that on the Plaza de España four hundred Assault Guards had surrendered and handed their arms to the Anarchists; also the news was vaguely filtering through that in the suburbs (mainly working-class quarters) the CNT were in control. It looked as though we were winning. But the same evening Kopp sent for me and, with a grave face, told me that according to information he had just received the Government was about to outlaw the POUM and declare a state of war upon it. The news gave me a shock. It was the first glimpse I had had of the interpretation that was likely to be put upon this affair later on. I dimly foresaw that when the fighting ended the entire blame would be laid upon the POUM, which was the weakest party and therefore the most suitable scapegoat. And meanwhile our local neutrality was at an end. If the Government declared war upon us we had no choice but to defend ourselves, and here at the Executive building we could be certain that the Assault Guards next door would get orders to attack us. Our only chance was to attack them first. Kopp was waiting for orders on the telephone, if we heard definitely that the POUM was outlawed we must make preparations at once to seize the Café Moka.

I remember the long, nightmarish evening that we spent in fortifying the building. We locked the steel curtains across the front entrance and behind them built a barricade of slabs of stone left behind by the workmen who had been making some alterations. We went over our stock of weapons. Counting the six rifles that were on the roof of the Poliorama opposite, we had twenty-one rifles, one of them defective, about fifty rounds of ammunition for each rifle, and a few dozen bombs, otherwise nothing except a few pistols and revolvers. About a dozen men, mostly Germans, had volunteered for the attack on the Café Moka, if it came off. We should attack from the roof, of course, some time in the small hours, and take them by surprise; they were more numerous, but our morale was better, and no doubt we could storm the place, though people were bound to be killed in doing so. We had no food in the building except a few slabs of chocolate, and the rumour had gone round that 'they' were going to cut off the water supply. (Nobody knew who 'they' were. It might be the Government that controlled the waterworks, or it might be the CNT – nobody knew.) We spent a long time filling up every basin in the lavatories, every bucket we could lay hands on, and, finally, the fifteen beer bottles, now empty, which the Assault Guards had given to Kopp.

I was in a ghastly frame of mind and dog-tired after about sixty hours without much sleep. It was now late into the night. People were sleeping all over the floor behind the barricade downstairs. Upstairs there was a small room, with a sofa in it, which we intended to use as a dressing-station, though, needless to say, we discovered that there was neither iodine nor bandages in the building. My wife had come down from the hotel in case a nurse should be needed. I lay down on the sofa, feeling that I would like half an hour's rest before the attack on the 'Moka', in which I should presumably be killed. I remember the intolerable discomfort caused by my pistol, which was strapped to my belt and sticking into the small of my back. And the next thing I remember is waking up with a jerk to find my wife standing beside me. It was broad daylight, nothing had happened, the Government had not declared war on the POUM, the water had not been cut off, and except for the sporadic firing in the streets everything was normal. My wife said that she had not had the heart to wake me and had slept in an armchair in one of the front rooms.

That afternoon there was a kind of armistice. The firing died away and with surprising suddenness the streets filled with people. A few shops began to pull up their shutters, and the market was packed with a huge crowd clamouring for food, though the stalls were almost empty. It was noticeable, however, that the trams did not start running. The Assault Guards were still behind their barricades in the 'Moka'; on neither side were the fortified buildings evacuated. Everyone was rushing round and trying to buy food. And on every side you heard the same anxious questions: 'Do you think it's stopped? Do you think it's going to start again?' 'It' – the fighting – was now thought of as some kind of natural calamity, like a hurricane or an earthquake, which was happening to us all alike and which we had no power of stopping. And sure enough, almost immediately – I suppose there must really have been several hours' truce, but they seemed more like minutes than hours – a sudden crash of rifle-fire, like a June cloudburst, sent everyone scurrying; the steel shutters snapped into place, the streets emptied like magic, the barricades were manned, and 'it' had started again.

I went back to my post on the roof with a feeling of concentrated disgust and fury. When you are taking part in events like these you are, I suppose, in a small way, making history, and you ought by rights to feel like an historical character. But you never do, because at such times the physical details always outweigh everything else. Throughout the fighting I never made the correct 'analysis' of the situation that was so glibly made by journalists hundreds of miles away. What I was chiefly thinking about was not the rights and wrongs of the miserable internecine scrap, but simply the discomfort and boredom of sitting day and night on that intolerable roof, and the hunger which was growing worse and worse – for none of us had had a proper meal since Monday. It was in my mind all the while that I should have to go back to the front as soon as this business was over. It was infuriating. I had been a hundred and fifteen days in the line and had come back to Barcelona ravenous for a bit of rest and comfort; and instead I had to spend my time sitting on a roof opposite Assault Guards as bored as myself, who periodically waved to me and assured me that they were 'workers' (meaning that they hoped I would not shoot them), but who would certainly open fire if they got the order to do so. If this was history it did not feel like it. It was more like a bad period at the front, when men were short and we had to do abnormal hours of guard-duty; instead of being heroic one just had to stay at one's post, bored, dropping with sleep and completely uninterested as to what it was all about.

Inside the hotel, among the heterogeneous mob who for the most part had not dared to put their noses out of doors, a horrible atmosphere of suspicion had grown up. Various people were infected with spy mania and were creeping round whispering that everyone else was a spy of the Communists, or the Trotskyists, or the Anarchists, or whatnot. The fat Russian agent was cornering all the foreign refugees in turn and explaining plausibly that this whole affair was an Anarchist plot. I watched him with some interest, for it was the first time that I had seen a person whose profession was telling lies – unless one counts journalists. There was something repulsive in the parody of smart hotel life that was still going on behind shuttered windows amid the rattle of rifle-fire. The front dining room had been abandoned after a bullet came through the window and chipped a pillar, and the guests were crowded into a darkish room at the back, where there were never quite enough tables to go round. The waiters were reduced in numbers – some of them were CNT members and had joined in the general strike – and had dropped their boiled shirts for the time being, but meals were still being served with a pretence of ceremony. There was, however, practically nothing to eat. On that Thursday night the principal dish at dinner was *one* sardine each. The hotel had had no bread for days, and even the wine was running so low that we were drinking older and older wines at higher and higher prices. This shortage of food went on for several days after the fighting was over. Three days running, I remember, my wife and I breakfasted off a little piece of goat's-milk cheese with no bread and nothing to drink. The only thing that was plentiful was oranges. The French lorry drivers brought quantities of their oranges into the hotel. They were a tough-looking bunch; they had with them some flashy Spanish girls and a huge porter in a black blouse. At any other time the little snob of an hotel manager would have done his best to make them uncomfortable, in fact would have refused to have them on the premises, but at present they were popular because, unlike the rest of us, they had a private store of bread which everyone was trying to cadge from them.

I spent that final night on the roof, and the next day it did really look as though the fighting was coming to an end. I do not think there was much firing that day – the Friday. No one seemed to know for certain whether the troops from Valencia were really coming; they arrived that evening, as a matter of fact. The Government was broadcasting half-soothing, half-threatening messages, asking everyone to go home and saying that after a certain hour anyone found carrying arms would be arrested. Not much attention was paid to the Government's broadcasts, but everywhere the people were fading away from the barricades. I have no doubt that it was mainly the food shortage that was responsible. From every side you heard the same remark: 'We have no more food, we must go back to work.' On the other hand the Assault Guards, who could count on getting their rations so long as there was any food in the town, were able to stay at their posts. By the afternoon the streets were almost normal, though the deserted barricades were still standing; the Ramblas were thronged with people, the shops nearly all open, and – most reassuring of all – the trams that had stood so long in frozen blocks jerked into motion and began running. The Assault Guards were still holding the Café Moka and had not taken down their barricades, but some of them brought chairs out and sat on the pavement with their rifles across their knees. I winked at one of them as I went past and got a not unfriendly grin; he recognized me, of course. Over the Telephone Exchange the Anarchist flag had been hauled down and only the Catalan flag was flying. That meant that the workers were definitely beaten; I realized – though, owing to my political ignorance, not so clearly as I ought to have done – that when the Government felt more sure of itself there would be reprisals. But at the time I was not interested in that aspect of things. All I felt was a profound relief that the devilish din of firing was over, and that one could buy some food and have a bit of rest and peace before going back to the front.

It must have been late that evening that the troops from Valencia first appeared in the streets. They were Assault Guards, another formation similar to the local Assault Guards, the hated Civil Guards and the Carabineros (i.e. a formation intended primarily for police work), and the picked troops of the Republic. Quite suddenly they seemed to spring up out of the ground;

you saw them everywhere patrolling the streets in groups of ten – tall men in grey or blue uniforms, with long rifles slung over their shoulders, and a sub-machine gun to each group. Meanwhile there was a delicate job to be done. The six rifles which we had used for the guard in the observatory towers were still lying there, and by hook or by crook we had got to get them back to the POUM building. It was only a question of getting them across the street. They were part of the regular armoury of the building, but to bring them into the street was to contravene the Government's order, and if we were caught with them in our hands we should certainly be arrested – worse, the rifles would be confiscated. With only twenty-one rifles in the building we could not afford to lose six of them. After a lot of discussion as to the best method, a red-haired Spanish boy and myself began to smuggle them out. It was easy enough to dodge the Valencian Assault Guard patrols; the danger was the local Assault Guards in the 'Moka', who were well aware that we had rifles in the observatory and might give the show away if they saw us carrying them across. Each of us partially undressed and slung a rifle over the left shoulder, the butt under the armpit, the barrel down the trouser-leg. It was unfortunate that they were long Mausers. Even a man as tall as I am cannot wear a long Mauser down his trouser-leg without discomfort. It was an intolerable job getting down the corkscrew staircase of the observatory with a completely rigid left leg. Once in the street, we found that the only way to move was with extreme slowness, so slowly that you did not have to bend your knees. Outside the picture-house I saw a group of people staring at me with great interest as I crept along at tortoise-speed. I have often wondered what they thought was the matter with me. Wounded in the war, perhaps. However, all the rifles were smuggled across without incident.

Next day the Valencian Assault Guards were every-where, walking the streets like conquerors. There was no doubt that the Government was simply making a display of force in order to overawe a population which it already knew would not resist; if there had been any real fear of further outbreaks the Valencian Assault Guards would have been kept in barracks and not scattered through the streets in small bands. They were splendid troops, much the best I had seen in Spain, and, though I suppose they were in a sense 'the enemy', I could not help liking the look of them. But it was with a sort of amazement that I watched them strolling to and fro. I was used to the ragged, scarcely-armed militia on the Aragón front, and I had not known that the Republic possessed troops like these. It was not only that they were picked men physically, it was their weapons that most astonished me. All of them were armed with brand new rifles of the type known as 'the Russian rifle' (these rifles were sent to Spain by the USSR, but were, I believe, manufactured in America). I examined one of them. It was a far from perfect rifle, but vastly better than the dreadful old blunderbusses we had at the front. The Valencian Assault Guards had one sub-machine gun between ten men and an auto-matic pistol each; we at the front had approximately one machine-gun between fifty men, and as for pistols and revolvers, you could only procure them illegally. As a matter of fact, though I had not noticed it till now, it was the same everywhere. The Assault Guards and Carabineros, who were not intended for the front at all, were better armed and far better clad than ourselves. I suspect it is the same in all wars – always the same contrast between the sleek police in the rear and the ragged soldiers in the line. On the whole the Valencian Assault Guards got on very well with the population after the first day or two. On the first day there was a certain amount of trouble because some of them – acting on instructions, I suppose – began behaving in a provocative manner. Bands of them boarded trams, searched the passengers, and, if they had CNT membership cards in their pockets, tore them up and stamped on them. This led to scuffles with armed Anarchists, and one or two people were killed. Very soon, however, the Valencian Assault Guards dropped their conquering air and relations became more friendly. It was noticeable that most of them had picked up a girl after a day or two.

The Barcelona fighting had given the Valencia Government the long-wanted excuse to assume fuller control of Catalonia. The workers' militias were to be broken up and redistributed among the Popular Army. The Spanish Republican flag was flying all over Barcelona – the first time I had seen it, I think, except over a Fascist trench. In the working-class quarters the barricades were being pulled down, rather fragmentarily for it is a lot easier to build a barricade than to put the stones back. Outside the PSUC buildings the barricades were allowed to remain standing, and indeed many were standing as late as June. The Assault Guards were still occupying strategic points. Huge seizures of arms were being made from CNT strongholds, though I have no doubt a good many escaped seizure. *La Batalla* was still appearing, but it was censored until the front page was almost completely blank. The PSUC papers were uncensored and were publishing inflammatory articles demanding the suppression of the POUM. The POUM was declared to be a disguised Fascist organization, and a cartoon representing the POUM as a figure slipping off a mask marked with the hammer and sickle and revealing a hideous, maniacal face marked with the swastika, was being circulated all over the town by PSUC agents. Evidently the official version of the Barcelona fighting was already fixed upon: it was to be represented as a 'fifth column' Fascist rising engineered solely by the POUM.

In the hotel the horrible atmosphere of suspicion and hostility had grown worse now that the fighting was over. In the face of the accusations that were being flung about it was impossible to remain neutral. The posts were working again, the foreign Communist papers were beginning to arrive, and their accounts of the fighting were not only violently partisan but, of course, wildly inaccurate as to facts. I think some of the Communists on the spot, who had seen what was actually happening, were dismayed by the interpretation that was being put upon events, but naturally they had to stick to their own side. Our Communist friend approached me once again and asked me whether I would not transfer into the International Column.

I was rather surprised. 'Your papers are saying I'm a Fascist,' I said. 'Surely I should be politically suspect, coming from the POUM.'

'Oh, that doesn't matter. After all, you were only acting under orders.'

I had to tell him that after this affair I could not join any Communist-controlled unit. Sooner or later it might mean being used against the Spanish working class. One could not tell when this kind of thing would break out again, and if I had to use my rifle at all in such an affair I would use it on the side of the working class and not against them. He was very decent about it. But from now on the whole atmosphere was changed. You could not, as before, 'agree to differ' and have drinks with a man who was supposedly your political opponent. There were some ugly wrangles in the hotel lounge. Meanwhile the jails were already full and overflowing. After the fighting was over the Anarchists had, of course, released their prisoners, but the Assault Guards had not released theirs, and most of them were thrown into prison and kept there without trial, in many cases for months on end. As usual, completely innocent people were being arrested owing to police bungling. I mentioned earlier that Douglas Thompson was wounded about the beginning of April. Afterwards we had lost touch with him, as usually happened when a man was wounded, for wounded men were frequently moved from one hospital to another.

Actually he was at Tarragona hospital and was sent back to Barcelona about the time when the fighting started. On the Tuesday morning I met him in the street, considerably bewildered by the firing that was going on all round. He asked the question everyone was asking:

'What the devil is this all about?'

I explained as well as I could. Thompson said promptly:

'I'm going to keep out of this. My arm's still bad. I shall go back to my hotel and stay there.'

He went back to his hotel, but unfortunately (how important it is in street-fighting to understand the local geography!) it was an hotel in a part of the town controlled by the Assault Guards. The place was raided and Thompson was arrested, flung into jail, and kept for eight days in a cell so full of people that nobody had room to lie down. There were many similar cases. Numerous foreigners with doubtful political records were on the run, with the police on their track and in constant fear of denunciation. It was worst for the Italians and Germans, who had no passports and were generally wanted by the secret police in their own countries. If they were arrested they were liable to be deported to France, which might mean being sent back to Italy or Germany, where God knew what horrors were awaiting them. One or two foreign women hurriedly regularized their position by 'marrying' Spaniards. A German girl who had no papers at all dodged the police by posing for several days as a man's mistress. I remember the look of shame and misery on the poor girl's face when I accidentally bumped into her coming out of the man's bedroom. Of course she was not his mistress, but no doubt she thought I thought she was. You had all the while a hateful feeling that someone hitherto your friend might be denouncing you to the secret police. The long nightmare of the fighting, the noise, the lack of food and sleep, the mingled strain and boredom of sitting on the roof and wondering whether in another minute I should be shot myself or be obliged to shoot somebody else had put my nerves on edge. I had got to the point when every time a door banged I grabbed for my pistol. On the Saturday morning there was an uproar of shots outside and everyone cried out: 'It's starting again!' I ran into the street to find that it was only some Valencian Assault Guards shooting a mad dog. No one who was in Barcelona then, or for months later, will forget the horrible atmosphere produced by fear, suspicion, hatred, censored newspapers, crammed jails, enormous food queues and prowling gangs of armed men.

I have tried to give some idea of what it felt like to be in the middle of the Barcelona fighting; yet I do not suppose I have succeeded in conveying much of the strangeness of that time. One of the things that stick in my mind when I look back is the casual contacts one made at the time, the sudden glimpses of non-combatants to whom the whole thing was simply a meaningless uproar. I remember the fashionably-dressed woman I saw strolling down the Ramblas, with a shopping-basket over her arm and leading a white poodle, while the rifles cracked and roared a street or two away. It is conceivable that she was deaf. And the man I saw rushing across the completely empty Plaza de Cataluña, brandishing a white handkerchief in each hand. And the large party of people all dressed in black who kept trying for about an hour to cross the Plaza de Cataluña and always failing. Every time they emerged from the side street at the corner the PSUC machine-gunners in the Hotel Colón opened fire and drove them back – I don't know why, for they were obviously unarmed. I have since thought that they may have been a funeral party. And the little man who acted as caretaker at the museum over the Poliorama and who seemed to regard the whole affair as a social occasion. He was so pleased to have the English visiting him – the English were so *simpático*, he said. He hoped we would all come and see him again when the trouble was over; as a matter of fact I did go and see him. And the other little man, sheltering in a doorway, who jerked his head in a pleased manner towards the hell of firing on the Plaza de Cataluña and said (as though remarking that it was a fine morning): 'So we've got the nineteenth of July back again!' And the people in the shoe-shop who were making my marching-boots. I went there before the fighting, after it was over, and, for a very few minutes, during the brief armistice on 5 May. It was an expensive shop, and the shop-people were UGT and may have been PSUC members – at any rate they were politically on the other side and they knew that I was serving with the POUM. Yet their attitude was completely indifferent. 'Such a pity, this kind of thing, isn't it? And so bad for business. What a pity it doesn't stop! As though there wasn't enough of that kind of thing at the front!' etc. etc. There must have been quantities of people, perhaps a majority of the inhabitants of Barcelona, who regarded the whole affair without a flicker of interest, or with no more interest than they would have felt in an air raid.

In this chapter I have described only my personal experiences. In *Appendix II* I discuss as best I can the larger issues – what actually happened and with what results, what were the rights and wrongs of the affair, and who if anyone was responsible. So much political capital has been made out of the Barcelona fighting that it is important to try and get a balanced view of it. An immense amount, enough to fill many books, has already been written on the subject, and I do not suppose I should exaggerate if I said that nine-tenths of it is untruthful. Nearly all the newspaper accounts published at the time were manufactured by journalists at a distance, and were not only inaccurate in their facts but intentionally misleading. As usual, only one side of the question has been allowed to get to the wider public. Like everyone who was in Barcelona at the time, I saw only what was happening in my immediate neighbourhood, but I saw and heard quite enough to be able to contradict many of the lies that have been circulated.

IX

It must have been three days after the Barcelona fighting ended that we returned to the front. After the fighting – more particularly after the slanging-match in the newspapers – it was difficult to think about this war in quite the same naïvely idealistic manner as before. I suppose there is no one who spent more than a few weeks in Spain without being in some degree disillusioned. My mind went back to the newspaper correspondent whom I had met my first day in Barcelona, and who said to me: 'This war is a racket the same as any other.' The remark had shocked me deeply, and at that time (December) I did not believe it was true; it was not true even now, in May; but it was becoming truer. The fact is that every war suffers a kind of progressive degradation with every month that it continues, because such things as individual liberty and a truthful press are simply not compatible with military efficiency.

We were still at Huesca, but they had placed us further to the right, opposite the Fascist redoubt which we had temporarily captured a few weeks earlier. I was now acting as *teniente* – corresponding to second-lieutenant in the British Army, I suppose – in command of about thirty men, English and Spanish. They had sent my name in for a regular commission; whether I should get it was uncertain. Previously the militia officers had refused to accept regular commissions, which meant extra pay and conflicted with the equalitarian ideas of the militia, but they were now obliged to do so. Benjamin had already been gazetted captain and Kopp was in process of being gazetted major. The Government could not, of course, dispense with the militia officers, but it was not confirming any of them in a higher rank than major, presumably in order to keep the higher commands for Regular Army officers and the new officers from the School of War. As a result, in our division, the 29th, and no doubt in many others, you had the queer temporary situation of the divisional commander, the brigade commanders and the battalion commanders all being majors.

There was not much happening at the front. The battle round the Jaca road had died away and did not begin again till mid-June. In our position the chief trouble was the snipers. The Fascist trenches were more than a hundred and fifty yards away, but they were on higher ground and were on two sides of us, our line forming a right-angle salient. The corner of the salient was a dangerous spot; there had always been a toll of sniper casualties there. From time to time the Fascists let fly at us with a rifle-grenade or some similar weapon. It made a ghastly crash – unnerving, because you could not hear it coming in time to dodge – but was not really dangerous; the hole it blew in the ground was no bigger than a wash-tub. The nights were pleasantly warm, the days blazing hot, the mosquitoes were becoming a nuisance, and in spite of the clean clothes we had brought from Barcelona we were almost immediately lousy. Out in the deserted orchards in no-man's-land the cherries were whitening on the trees. For two days there were torrential rains, the dugouts flooded and the parapet sank a foot; after that there were more days of digging out the sticky clay with the wretched Spanish spades which have no handles and bend like tin spoons.

They had promised us a trench-mortar for the company; I was looking forward to it greatly. At nights we patrolled as usual – more dangerous than it used to be, because the Fascist trenches were better manned and they had grown more alert; they had scattered tin cans just outside their wire and used to open up with the machine-guns when they heard a clank. In the daytime we sniped from no-man's-land. By crawling a hundred yards you could get to a ditch, hidden by tall grasses, which commanded a gap in the Fascist parapet. We had set up a rifle-rest in the ditch. If you waited long enough you generally saw a khaki-clad figure slip hurriedly across the gap. I had several shots. I don't know whether I hit anyone – it is most unlikely; I am a very poor shot with a rifle. But it was rather fun, the Fascists did not know where the shots were coming from, and I made sure I would get one of them sooner or later. However, the dog it was that died – a Fascist sniper got me instead. I had been about ten days at the front when it happened. The whole experience of being hit by a bullet is very interesting and I think it is worth describing in detail.

It was at the corner of the parapet, at five o'clock in the morning. This was always a dangerous time, because we had the dawn at our backs, and if you stuck your head above the parapet it was clearly outlined against the sky. I was talking to the sentries preparatory to changing the guard. Suddenly, in the very middle of saying something, I felt – it is very hard to describe what I felt, though I remember it with the utmost vividness.

Roughly speaking it was the sensation of being *at the centre* of an explosion. There seemed to be a loud bang and a blinding flash of light all round me, and I felt a tremendous shock – no pain, only a violent shock, such as you get from an electric terminal; with it a sense of utter weakness, a feeling of being stricken and shrivelled up to nothing. The sandbags in front of me receded into immense distance. I fancy you would feel much the same if you were struck by lightning. I knew immediately that I was hit, but because of the seeming bang and flash I thought it was a rifle nearby that had gone off accidentally and shot me. All this happened in a space of time much less than a second. The next moment my knees crumpled up and I was falling, my head hitting the ground with a violent bang which, to my relief, did not hurt. I had a numb, dazed feeling, a consciousness of being very badly hurt, but no pain in the ordinary sense.

The American sentry I had been talking to had started forward. 'Gosh'. Are you hit?' People gathered round. There was the usual fuss – 'Lift him up! Where's he hit? Get his shirt open!' etc. etc. The American called for a knife to cut my shirt open. I knew that there was one in my pocket and tried to get it out, but discovered that my right arm was paralysed. Not being in pain, I felt a vague satisfaction. This ought to please my wife, I thought; she had always wanted me to be wounded, which would save me from being killed when the great battle came. It was only now that it occurred to me to wonder where I was hit, and how badly: I could feel nothing, but I was conscious that the bullet had struck me somewhere in the front of the body. When I tried to speak I found that I had no voice, only a faint squeak, but at the second attempt I managed to ask where I was hit. In the throat, they said. Harry Webb, our stretcher-bearer, had brought a bandage and one of the little bottles of alcohol they gave us for field-dressings. As they lifted me up a lot of blood poured out of my mouth, and I heard a Spaniard behind me say that the bullet had gone clean through my neck. I felt the alcohol, which at ordinary times would sting like the devil, splash onto the wound as a pleasant coolness.

They laid me down again while somebody fetched a stretcher. As soon as I knew that the bullet had gone clean through my neck I took it for granted that I was done for. I had never heard of a man or an animal getting a bullet through the middle of the neck and surviving it. The blood was dribbling out of the corner of my mouth. 'The artery's gone,' I thought. I wondered how long you last when your carotid artery is cut; not many minutes, presumably. Everything was very blurry. There must have been about two minutes during which I assumed that I was killed. And that too was interesting – I mean it is interesting to know what your thoughts would be at such a time. My first thought, conventionally enough, was for my wife. My second was a violent resentment at having to leave this world which, when all is said and done, suits me so well. I had time to feel this very vividly. The stupid mischance infuriated me. The meaninglessness of it! To be bumped off, not even in battle, but in this stale corner of the trenches, thanks to a moment's carelessness! I thought, too, of the man who had shot me – wondered what he was like, whether he was a Spaniard or a foreigner, whether he knew he had got me, and so forth. I could not feel any resentment against him. I reflected that as he was a Fascist I would have killed him if I could, but that if he had been taken prisoner and brought before me at this moment I would merely have congratulated him on his good shooting. It may be, though, that if you were really dying your thoughts would be quite different.

They had just got me onto the stretcher when my paralysed right arm came to life and began hurting damnably. At the time I imagined that I must have broken it in falling; but the pain reassured me, for I knew that your sensations do not become more acute when you are dying. I began to feel more normal and to be sorry for the four poor devils who were sweating and slithering with the stretcher on their shoulders. It was a mile and a half to the ambulance, and vile going, over lumpy, slippery tracks. I knew what a sweat it was, having helped to carry a wounded man down a day or two earlier. The leaves of the silver poplars which, in places, fringed our trenches brushed against my face; I thought what a good thing it was to be alive in a world where silver poplars grow. But all the while the pain in my arm was diabolical, making me swear and then try not to swear, because every time I breathed too hard the blood bubbled out of my mouth.

The doctor re-bandaged the wound, gave me a shot of morphia, and sent me off to Siétamo. The hospitals at Siétamo were hurriedly constructed wooden huts where the wounded were, as a rule, only kept for a few hours before being sent on to Barbastro or Lérida. I was dopey from morphia but still in great pain, practically unable to move and swallowing blood constantly. It was typical of Spanish hospital methods that while I was in this state the untrained nurse tried to force the regulation hospital meal – a huge meal of soup, eggs, greasy stew and so forth – down my throat and seemed surprised when I would not take it. I asked for a cigarette, but this was one of the periods of tobacco famine and there was not a cigarette in the place. Presently two comrades who had got permission to leave the line for a few hours appeared at my bedside.

'Hullo! You're alive, are you? Good. We want your watch and your revolver and your electric torch. And your knife, if you've got one.'

They made off with all my portable possessions. This always happened when a man was wounded – everything he possessed was promptly divided up; quite rightly, for watches, revolvers, and so forth were precious at the front and if they went down the line in a wounded man's kit they were certain to be stolen somewhere on the way.

By the evening enough sick and wounded had

trickled in to make up a few ambulance-loads, and they
sent us on to Barbastro. What a journey! It used to be
said that in this war you got well if you were wounded
in the extremities, but always died of a wound in the
abdomen. I now realised why. No one who was liable
to bleed internally could have survived those miles of
jolting over metal roads that had been smashed to
pieces by heavy lorries and never repaired since the war
began. Bang, bump, wallop! It took me back to my
early childhood and a dreadful thing called the Wiggle-
Woggle at the White City Exhibition. They had for-
gotten to tie us into the stretchers. I had enough
strength in my left arm to hang on, but one poor wretch
was spilt onto the floor and suffered God knows what
agonies. Another, a walking case who was sitting in
the corner of the ambulance, vomited all over the place.
The hospital in Barbastro was very crowded, the beds
so close together that they were almost touching. Next
morning they loaded a number of us onto the hospital
train and sent us down to Lérida.

I was five or six days in Lérida. It was a big hospital,
with sick, wounded, and ordinary civilian patients more
or less jumbled up together. Some of the men in my
ward had frightful wounds. In the next bed to me there
was a youth with black hair who was suffering from
some disease or other and was being given medicine
that made his urine as green as emerald. His bed-
bottle was one of the sights of the ward. An English-
speaking Dutch Communist, having heard that there
was an Englishman in the hospital, befriended me and
brought me English newspapers. He had been terribly

wounded in the October fighting, and had somehow managed to settle down at Lérida hospital and had married one of the nurses. Thanks to his wound, one of his legs had shrivelled till it was no thicker than my arm. Two militia men on leave, whom I had met my first week at the front, came in to see a wounded friend and recognized me. They were kids of about eighteen. They stood awkwardly beside my bed, trying to think of something to say, and then, as a way of demonstrating that they were sorry I was wounded, suddenly took all the tobacco out of their pockets, gave it to me, and fled before I could give it back. How typically Spanish! I discovered afterwards that you could not buy tobacco anywhere in the town and what they had given me was a week's ration.

After a few days I was able to get up and walk about with my arm in a sling. For some reason it hurt much more when it hung down. I also had, for the time being, a good deal of internal pain from the damage I had done myself in falling, and my voice had disappeared almost completely, but I never had a moment's pain from the bullet wound itself. It seems this is usually the case. The tremendous shock of a bullet prevents sensation locally; a splinter of shell or bomb, which is jagged and usually hits you less hard, would probably hurt like the devil. There was a pleasant garden in the hospital grounds, and in it was a pool with goldfishes and some small dark grey fish – bleak, I think. I used to sit watching them for hours. The way things were done at Lérida gave me an insight into the hospital system on the Aragón front – whether it was the same on other fronts I do not know. In some ways the hospitals were very good. The doctors were able men and there seemed to be no shortage of drugs and equipment. But there were two bad faults on account of which, I have no doubt, hundreds or thousands of men have died who might have been saved.

One was the fact that all the hospitals anywhere near the front line were used more or less as casualty clearing-stations. The result was that you got no treatment there unless you were too badly wounded to be moved. In theory most of the wounded were sent straight to Barcelona or Tarragona, but owing to the lack of transport they were often a week or ten days in getting there. They were kept hanging about at Siétam, Barbastro, Monzón, Lérida, and other places, and meanwhile they were getting no treatment except an occasional clean bandage, sometimes not even that. Men with dreadful shell wounds, smashed bones and so forth, were swathed in a sort of casing made of bandages and plaster of Paris; a description of the wound was written in pencil on the outside, and as a rule the casing was not removed till the man reached Barcelona or Tarragona ten days later. It was almost impossible to get one's wound examined on the way; the few doctors could not cope with the work, and they simply walked hurriedly past your bed, saying. 'Yes, yes, they'll attend to you at Barcelona.' There were always rumours that the hospital train was leaving for Barcelona *mañana*. The other fault was the lack of competent nurses. Apparently there was no supply of trained nurses in Spain, perhaps because before the war this work was done chiefly by nuns. I have no complaint against the Spanish nurses, they always treated me with the greatest kindness, but there is no doubt that they were terribly ignorant. All of them knew how to take a temperature, and some of them knew how to tie a bandage, but that was about all. The result was that men who were too ill to fend for themselves were often shamefully neglected. The nurses would let a man remain constipated for a week on end, and they seldom washed those who were too weak to wash themselves. I remember one poor devil with a smashed arm telling me that he had been three weeks without having his face washed. Even beds were left unmade for days together. The food in all the hospitals was very good – too good, indeed. Even more in Spain than elsewhere it seemed to be the tradition to stuff sick people with heavy food. At Lérida the meals were terrific. Breakfast, at about six in the morning, con-sisted of soup, an omelette, stew, bread, white wine, and coffee, and lunch was even larger – this at a time when most of the civil population was seriously under-fed. Spaniards seem not to recognize such a thing as a light diet. They give the same food to sick people as to well ones – always the same rich, greasy cookery, with everything sodden in olive oil.

One morning it was announced that the men in my ward were to be sent down to Barcelona today. I managed to send a wire to my wife, telling her that I was coming, and presently they packed us into buses and took us down to the station. It was only when the train was actually starting that the hospital orderly who travelled with us casually let fall that we were not going to Barcelona after all, but to Tarragona. I suppose the engine-driver had changed his mind. 'Just like Spain!' I thought. But it was very Spanish, too, that they agreed to hold up the train while I sent another wire, and more Spanish still that the wire never got there.

They had put us into ordinary third-class carriages with wooden seats, and many of the men were badly wounded and had only got out of bed for the first time that morning. Before long, what with the heat and the jolting, half of them were in a state of collapse and several vomited on the floor. The hospital orderly threaded his way among the corpse-like forms that sprawled everywhere, carrying a large goatskin bottle full of water which he squirted into this mouth or that. It was beastly water; I remember the taste of it still. We got into Tarragona as the sun was getting low. The line runs along the shore a stone's throw from the sea. As our train drew into the station a troop-train full of men from the International Column was drawing out, and a knot of people on the bridge were waving to them. It was a very long train, packed to bursting-point with men, with field-guns lashed on the open trucks and more men clustering round the guns. I remember with peculiar vividness the spectacle of that train passing in the yellow evening light; window after window full of dark, smiling faces, the long tilted barrels of the guns, the scarlet scarves fluttering – all this gliding slowly past us against a turquoise-coloured sea.

'*Estranjeros* – foreigners,' said someone. 'They're Italians.'

Obviously they were Italians. No other people could have grouped themselves so picturesquely or returned the salutes of the crowd with so much grace – a grace that was none the less because about half the men on the train were drinking out of up-ended wine bottles. We heard afterwards that these were some of the troops who won the great victory at Guadalajara in March; they had been on leave and were being transferred to the Aragón front. Most of them, I am afraid, were killed at Huesca only a few weeks later. The men who were well enough to stand had moved across the carriage to cheer the Italians as they went past. A crutch waved out of the window; bandaged forearms made the Red Salute. It was like an allegorical picture of war; the trainload of fresh men gliding proudly up the line, the maimed men sliding slowly down, and all the while the guns on the open trucks making one's heart leap as guns always do, and reviving that pernicious feeling, so difficult to get rid of, that war *is* glorious after all.

The hospital at Tarragona was a very big one and full of wounded from all fronts. What wounds one saw there! They had a way of treating certain wounds which I suppose was in accordance with the latest medical practice, but which was peculiarly horrible to look at. This was to leave the wound completely open and unbandaged, but protected from flies by a net of butter-muslin, stretched over wires. Under the muslin you would see the red jelly of a half-healed wound. There was one man wounded in the face and throat who had his head inside a sort of spherical helmet of butter-muslin; his mouth was closed up and he breathed through a little tube that was fixed between his lips. Poor devil, he looked so lonely wandering to and fro, looking at you through his muslin cage and unable to speak. I was three or four days at Tarragona. My strength was coming back, and one day, by going slowly, I managed to walk down as far as the beach. It was queer to see the seaside life going on almost as usual; the smart cafés along the promenade and the plump local bourgeoisie bathing and sunning themselves in deckchairs as though there had not been a war within a thousand miles. Nevertheless, as it happened, I saw a bather drowned, which one would have thought impossible in that shallow and tepid sea.

Finally, eight or nine days after leaving the front, I had my wound examined. In the surgery where newly-arrived cases were examined, doctors with huge pairs of shears were hacking away the breast-plates of plaster in which men with smashed ribs, collar bones and so forth had been cased at the dressing-stations behind the line; out of the neck-hole of the huge clumsy breast-plate you would see protruding an anxious, dirty face, scrubby with a week's beard. The doctor, a brisk, handsome man of about thirty, sat me down in a chair, grasped my tongue with a piece of rough gauze, pulled it out as far as it would go, thrust a dentist's mirror down my throat and told me to say 'Eh!' After doing this till my tongue was bleeding and my eyes running with water, he told me that one vocal cord was paralysed.

'When shall I get my voice back?' I said.

'Your voice? Oh, you'll never get your voice back,' he said cheerfully.

However, he was wrong, as it turned out. For about two months I could not speak much above a whisper, but after that my voice became normal rather suddenly, the other vocal cord having 'compensated'. The pain in my arm was due to the bullet having pierced a bunch of nerves at the back of the neck. It was a shooting pain like neuralgia, and it went on hurting continuously for about a month, especially at night, so that I did not get much sleep. The fingers of my right hand were also semi-paralysed. Even now, five months afterwards, my forefinger is still numb – a queer effect for a neck wound to have.

The wound was a curiosity in a small way and various doctors examined it with much clicking of tongues and *'Qué suerte! Qué suerte!'* One of them told me with an air of authority that the bullet had missed the artery by 'about a millimetre'. I don't know how he knew. No one I met at this time – doctors, nurses, *practicantes*, or fellow-patients – failed to assure me that a man who is hit through the neck and survives it is the luckiest creature alive. I could not help thinking that it would be even luckier not to be hit at all.

Looking Back on the Spanish War

(extract taken from 'Looking Back on the Spanish War', 1942, from *Orwell in Spain*.)

The outcome of the Spanish War was settled in London, Paris, Rome, Berlin – at any rate not in Spain. After the summer of 1937 those with eyes in their heads realized that the Government could not win the war unless there was some profound change in the international set-up, and in deciding to fight on Negrín and the others may have been partly influenced by the expectation that the world war which actually broke out in 1939 was coming in 1938. The much-publicized disunity on the Government side was not a main cause of defeat. The Government militias were hurriedly raised, ill-armed and unimaginative in their military outlook, but they would have been the same if complete political agreement had existed from the start. At the outbreak of war the average Spanish factory-worker did not even know how to fire a rifle (there had never been universal conscription in Spain), and the traditional pacifism of the Left was a great handicap. The thousands of foreigners who served in Spain made good infantry, but there were very few experts of any kind among them. The Trotskyist thesis that the war could have been won if the revolution had not been sabotaged was probably false. To nationalize factories, demolish churches, and issue revolutionary manifestos would not have made the armies more efficient. The Fascists won because they were the stronger; they had modern arms and the others hadn't. No political strategy could offset that.

The most baffling thing in the Spanish War was the behaviour of the great powers. The war was actually won for Franco by the Germans and Italians, whose motives were obvious enough. The motives of France and Britain are less easy to understand. In 1936 it was clear to everyone that if Britain would only help the Spanish Government, even to the extent of a few million pounds' worth of arms, Franco would collapse and German strategy would be severely dislocated. By that time one did not need to be a clairvoyant to foresee that war between Britain and Germany was coming; one could even foretell within a year or two when it would come. Yet in the most mean, cowardly, hypocritical way the British ruling class did all they could to hand Spain over to Franco and the Nazis. Why? Because they were pro-Fascist, was the obvious answer. Undoubtedly they were, and yet when it came to the final showdown they chose to stand up to Germany. It is still very uncertain what plan they acted on in backing Franco, and they may have had no clear plan at all. Whether the British ruling class are wicked or merely stupid is one of the most difficult questions of our time, and at certain moments a very important question. As to the Russians, their motives in the Spanish War are completely inscrutable. Did they, as the pinks believed, intervene in Spain in order to defend democracy and thwart the Nazis? Then why did they intervene on such a niggardly scale and finally leave Spain in the lurch? Or did they, as the Catholics maintained, intervene in order to foster revolution in Spain? Then why did they do all in their power to crush the Spanish revolutionary movements, defend private property and hand power to the middle class as against the working class? Or did they, as the Trotskyists suggested, intervene simply in order to *prevent* a Spanish revolution? Then why not have backed Franco? Indeed, their actions are most easily explained if one assumes that they were acting on several contradictory motives. I believe that in the future we shall come to feel that Stalin's foreign policy, instead of being so diabolically clever as it is claimed to be, has been merely opportunistic and stupid. But at any rate, the Spanish Civil War demonstrated that the Nazis knew what they were doing and their opponents did not. The war was fought at a low technical level and its major strategy was very simple. That side which had arms would win. The Nazis and the Italians gave arms to their Spanish Fascist friends, and the western democracies and the Russians didn't give arms to those who should have been their friends. So the Spanish Republic perished, having 'gained what no republic missed'.

Whether it was right, as all left-wingers in other countries undoubtedly did, to encourage the Spaniards to go on fighting when they could not win is a question hard to answer. I myself think it was right, because I believe that it is better even from the point of view of survival to fight and be conquered than to surrender without fighting. The effects on the grand strategy of the struggle against Fascism cannot be assessed yet. The ragged, weaponless armies of the Republic held out for two and a half years, which was undoubtedly longer than their enemies expected. But whether that dislocated the Fascist time-table, or whether, on the other hand, it merely postponed the major war and gave the Nazis extra time to get their war machine into trim, is still uncertain.

THE STORY OF PENGUIN CLASSICS

Before 1946 ... 'Classics' are mainly the domain of academics and students, without readable editions for everyone else. This all changes when a little-known classicist, E. V. Rieu, presents Penguin founder Allen Lane with the translation of Homer's *Odyssey* that he has been working on and reading to his wife Nelly in his spare time.

1946 *The Odyssey* becomes the first Penguin Classic published, and promptly sells three million copies. Suddenly, classic books are no longer for the privileged few.

1950s Rieu, now series editor, turns to professional writers for the best modern, readable translations, including Dorothy L. Sayers's *Inferno* and Robert Graves's *The Twelve Caesars*, which revives the salacious original.

1960s The Classics are given the distinctive black jackets that have remained a constant throughout the series's various looks. Rieu retires in 1964, hailing the Penguin Classics list as 'the greatest educative force of the 20th century'.

1970s A new generation of translators arrives to swell the Penguin Classics ranks, and the list grows to encompass more philosophy, religion, science, history and politics.

1980s The Penguin American Library joins the Classics stable, with titles such as *The Last of the Mohicans* safeguarded. Penguin Classics now offers the most comprehensive library of world literature available.

1990s The launch of Penguin Audiobooks brings the classics to a listening audience for the first time, and in 1999 the launch of the Penguin Classics website takes them online to a larger global readership than ever before.

The 21st Century Penguin Classics are rejacketed for the first time in nearly twenty years. This world famous series now consists of more than 1300 titles, making the widest range of the best books ever written available to millions – and constantly redefining the meaning of what makes a 'classic'.

The Odyssey continues ...

The best books ever written

PENGUIN CLASSICS

SINCE 1946

Find out more at www.penguinclassics.com